Multiples of Pulchritude

Multiples of Pulchritude

The Debut

Rebecca Mummery

To order additional copies of this book, contact:
Xlibris Corporation
0-800-644-6988
www.xlibrispublishing.co.uk
Orders@xlibrispublishing.co.uk
301475

Contents

Dedications

To my father and my Nan who have supported me throughout my illness, and who have supported me throughout the writing process.

To my former Mental Health doctor, Dr. Reddy, who suggested that instead of keeping a journal for all my thoughts, that I channel my focus through poetry. And as well as not being able to enter the fantastic world of poetry, I would also not have had the courage nor the confidence, to attempt poetry for children, if he had not encouraged me to do so.

To the C.I.T team, whose support and help has been phenomenal. In particular, to both my counsellors, Jenny and Jane, who have and continue to take me out to places on a weekly basis. And to my current doctor, Dr. "Tony", who has also supported me, and helps me make sense of my thoughts.

(Adult Poetry)

A Beautiful Night upon the Sands

Night's gentle breath descends
upon the sands,
Making of them wispy flurries
upon low grounds,
And our feet become mottled
by miniscule golden matter,
And the ebbing of the tide lends
its shapeless hands,
To soak our feet into
brackish wine of Adam,
This crystalline of all waters;
sands weld with the seas;
Their shallow billows,
make a towering dance of water's
sorrow,
And the placid wind's breeze
smelt of salt,
Making of the sea a myriad
of rippling serenity,
And Adam's wine presides over
the creatures in its hold,
And a moon's light makes of
old sands some treasury gold,
The night is forever in the springtime
of life,
And moon's light cuts through our
skins,
To make of us half-dressed in light; a
silvery thing,
To make of us half-doused in moon's
expression,
And a deadened, gloomy, deathly
sea lessens,
When moon's artistry expression
makes of it shimmering beauty,

And watch how light and seas
and sands entwine,
it's forever long captured in the
eyes of mine,
I behold the true beauty of
this earth,
And it does not require our
working day,
Our hours of strenuous work
to be paid,
To both the sea and the sands,
as we come to this place,
With no sterling in our hands,
only with bare feet,
To stride across those timeless
sands,
And to watch the relationship
between moon, sand and sea,
It's what I came to see,
and this is the definition of
being free,
Of life's harrowing counterparts,
it is at night the beauty starts,
On this beach of dreams,
And to watch this relationship
between moon, sand and sea,
Is the duty of this night,
and to watch a moon's glow
Descend upon the stretch and
wave,
Making of the night,
a heavenly white,
a beautiful place.

A Bird with Wings

The world and its people,
though I am in some other
Most of the time . . .
though it does not make me
Anymore tough, a
person dealt fantasy with
Some life-long fine,
and that is to become
Some social bird,
but it is only in my own
Unmarred world, that I
can spread my bird wings,
It may appear something absurd,
but once cannot spread one's
In front of other things,
and I find myself in a cage-
Not a nest,
refrain from turning the page,
They say it is only best,
best for whom?

I remain solitary
in some people haunt or
Some other room,
and imprisonment was not
My policy,
in some ghastly place of melancholy!

A Day in the Life: Part I

Not a vestige of hope,
from an old man's chair,
The legs are crooked,
but he does not care.

A wooden chair's hull,
chipped and scratched,
Now a worthless antique,
playing host to one so detached.

The crumbling, light ceiling
will become the Heaven's for his strife,
The firmament to his sight,
the highest ambition of his kite!

The burning embers of the fire,
raging, feral flames of regret,
Now a block of darkness,
as the pendulum strikes "bed . . ."

A Day in the Life: Part II

As dawn pours over the roofs,
and interrogates a plaintive room,
A man whose character is aloof,
takes place in such piteous gloom.

The spirited-faced younger
generation,
Sang hymns and prayers for the
man,
His eyes were devoid of fervour,
replaced with eyes that stung.

An artist created him upon
canvas,
With a mixture of hostility and
misery,
His hands were bereft of piety,
stood in lieu with ones that destroyed
history.

As dawn drips over the roofs,
and interrogates a four-poster bed,
A man whose character is aloof,
is in slumber so deep,
He is dead.

A Distance Far

Dirty pollution sounds
on those fallacy roads,
Those awful, narrow grounds,
that do not shine of erosion.

Concrete will not lead you
anywhere,
Not unto higher truth,
the guitar was fulfilling
separate functions,
Before it became a lute,
and so earthy grounds
Will always serve us the
same,
But concrete was the new,
and the new will serve us
with tales,
But never tales of the
truth.

I walked on foot to get here,
I did not cruise by car,
Bearing gifts of myrrh,
convenience is such,
It will not get you as far,
as gruelling hardship,
Something no deadly fumes
can mar.

Aegri Somnia

A sick man's dreams,
he cannot live them during
sleep's coma,
Though when awake in the
spotlight, filtered through the
blinds—the Sun beams,
And despite its visit not
making on the walls of eternal
duration,
Some positive, everlasting mural,
the spotlight evokes a
Sick man's dream from
conscious thought, the moment . . .

When he does not believe
he is sick.

All Men in Jeopardy

Runs like a ragged silk,
those impoverished men of hope,
Endless trails of ragged rope,
those resistance men of humane
ilk.

Treads like the feet of riot,
those impoverished men of hope,
To ground, that harshest of ropes,
those resistance men who remain
quiet,

God forbid, one man should lift
the tattered, twisted rope,
Once part of the legion of good hope,
now all hope is smothered by
hands holding the rope,
And all good resistance will quietly
shift,
Out of good men; impoverished
now by their lust for the rope . . .

I can only hope,
as one of those,
That he put back to the ground
his rope.

A Mind Dystopia

Everything I once was,
dispossessed,
Of life's euphoria,
the doctor's assessment,
My head's dystopia,
an utopia does not exist,
For real, or in sleep,
what my sleep exposes to me,
I am permitted to keep,
the disturbance I see.

Everything I once knew,
in-valid,
Of now, not erudition,
and of the colour of life's pallet,
Black oozing from mind's incision,
colour is not prevailing,
Life's complexion has been
drained like the sick,
Dark's temporary bruise,
of my life, it has stained thick,
And now, I'm left with nothing
to lose!

A Morning Realisation

I redressed the dark with
candlelight,
And wandered full of sprite,
to abandon the dark, cold night!

The kitchen floor was claret;
was red,
Not from I—I was not dead!

I am always sequestered
by my choice,
Until I heard some cry or voice,
And I became so still and poised!

I retired for some sleep
and wandered on an up stair
darkness,
The place of that which
mark us:
Faceless, bodiless figments!

And when the morn arrived,
I laughed,
I laughed so hard I cried,
The voice and blood was mine,
that cold, dark night—I died!

Aquila Non Capit Muscas

The face on your skin
glitters with façade,
And concealed within
your clenched fist, hand-made,
Is a crumpled sheet of foil.

You say you had captured
the moon one Winter's evening,
And that now the Sun relapses,
whilst moon inside your grasp is weeping,
But his tears walk out from *your* pores.

I found the ball of foil on the floor,
and heard you now held a
dandelion,
Crushed, its skin colour coloured your pores,
you have a soul of iron,
Liars weighed down with lies,
intentions gruesome as the silent moors.

The eagle does not catch flies,
he has bigger fish to fry,
Like I do not feed off peasants,
the fish cannot live on land,
Nor shock me with its presence,
and you did not catch the moon nor
Sun in their wrath of skies,
and . . .
I do not feed off lies!

A Shadow Journal: Some Extracts

Monday, they are
linking arms and brandishing them,
Eyes misinterpret on some,
and for all, not marred,
In distance short and distance far,
denying the opaque in resolute stance,
To make themselves upon
brick walls, flaunt and dance,
And there is no chance,
a new breed of effortless artists will close the show,
And make of shadows nothing
from the person they have flown.

Tuesday, they are
taking strides and revealing an outline,
Eyes interpret in mine,
an irregular cluster of silhouette stars,
And for all, not marred,
in distance short and distance far,
Stealing the bright from trees,
to make themselves upon the barks; an ever—changing disease,
And there is no seize,
from the clasping fingers,
However adamant our grasp,
Shadows; they forever withstand the test, and forever they linger.

Wednesday, they are
becoming large and small in fluctuating tease,
Eyes directed to the melting freeze,
And for all, not marred,
in distance short and distance far,
Robbing the opaque of a main role,
to make themselves upon carpet, a motion picture of charcoal,
And there is no parole,
of a stern-faced warden,
And he cannot arrest them,
or say how he caught them.

Thursday, they are
crouching in inhabited corners,
Sharing their art on both sides of walls that bore us,
And for all, not marred,
in distance short and distance far,
Taking away from an old wall, a finer shade,
to paint themselves upon the walls,
No existence feigned,
these are in parallel with one,
Or some object or solid thing,

A Well Respected Man vs. Fame

The man who works a mundane
work,
And his ears smile of the
radio they hear,
And the picturesque landscape
forever sleeps in his eyes,
And the flowers salute his
presence, before each one dies,
And the sun doth shine upon his
back so intensely,
It can only be a gesture
plucked out from its density,
And the men in high places
dismantle their top hats,
And old ladies abandon
the bench they once sat,
This is the life,
for one so respected,
But the errors are rife,
in one so infected,
With the trouble of the world,
a crying shame,
For the voice not sounded,
is a scream not heard,
And the difference with fame,
is they love to be infected,
For the money they squandered,
and life, they necked it.
That poison of life will kill them, sure
it will, but no one is pure,
not even our Bill,
Our well respected man.

A Winter's Valley

I

During this harsh night of a
Winter's reign
Of dour expression
riding through bare trees
So plain and
accompanying men so bedraggled
In delirium of mulled wine,
a bone-chilling breath of the
Winds, to them is aeon,
so supine those
Child progenies in snow,
and o' they do not know
The weather is but
the bane of a man's life,
Making of his speech
some hard ice, and
In a trice,
he becomes dead from
The cold,
eyes still widened, behold
The whole of the valley
in a tightly, clinging surplice,
As he does,
o' death upon death!
O' death to behold!

II

The wood clad trees make
a move to connect, just
Some overture of theirs
in which both their fears
Become as one,
bemoaning in linked arms,
Those sickeningly painful
branches,
Clinging to one another for
dear life,
O' my dear, nothing is
more than we hold dear,
Than this bitter night!
The debris of Autumn;
indecisive painted leaves,
They tend to the ground,
tend to their every need,
To be in company,
the only demonstration
Of Altruism you
will find here,
Wander adrift the
white floors mottled with Autumnal shades!
In humanly despair!

III

We allow the black
Winter,
To nourish us with idea
that we lead a lonely
Ghost
inside of us,
To all sorts of destinations dull,
a thrashing of snow that
To the flowers, it does null
their rainbow intentions
Of making of us—infection
of life's hope and delight,
To regain this infection,
with vanity plight,
Whores about the place
seeking sensual solace,
But a man's bed
is the grass,
Amassing in snow's deepness,
when he is dying; is dead,
Made so by the chill,
and he shall bequeath in a will,
A philistine legacy young,
not old!
For the young are taken by
the cold!

IV

O' a valley made nondescript
of colours and culture,
Indeed, the white blanket
is in itself—outstanding,
But it belittles true good,
true growth, and we
Cannot see the
trilling duet of bird souls,
Only of vultures
who reap the ground of
Their fellow brethren,
bought and sold to an
Air so candid,
brings to the foreground-
God's errors,
and evokes all terrors
Of that demon cold,
but as the bard,
I shall blast through the cold
with worth and words,
No matter how a breath bites hard,
but nonetheless, I shall reflect
When I am old!
O' that demonic, and harshest
of all winds cold!

An Ode to Despair

The forest I had step foot unto, dense,
unsettling and ten
Trees stood me on my knees, those
trees in pride, side by side,
Bark's as wide
as the prunish petal of the bodied
Delicate stem
that had died,
And the painfully narrow, towering trees
provoked my unease, carried no emerald
leaves
Of the days gone by, the primitive
bareness that identified
The Summer, the Spring, the child within
that awful thing they called the world
that had left us, and
All alone where flowers had ceased to grow, and
withered solemnly in frozen
Breath of the wind's lament,
where each endeavour to catch the sanity
Scratched through wide-growing eyes
was cruelly met with the distorted reality
Of each chimera, of eye's
deceit and lie, and it's shameful
Demise . . .
Nigh! The light parchment of the
Sky
Will become drenched in black ink
rapidly to sink amidst this
stark realisation that the
Despair has sent a kiss
straight to my heart!

Anxiety—An Insight

Lightsome strangers make a fearsome cavalcade;
they sought refuge in the bars, the clubs, and in town.
And I become infused in the banters and shrieks,
panic-stricken, and wall-bound.
And upon some bench, or solid ground,
I anchor my body against the sight and the sound.
My nerve-prompted twitches, derived from richest
anxiety, an intimidation and hostility against
all of humanity,
And this is permanence,
of which I am certain.

Asunder into Slumber

Orioles serenade me
into slumber,
Into asunder,
my stream of conscience,
On the purlieus of
maddening thoughts,
Are estuaries of solitude
bought,
With fatigue and suffocation,
and a numbing sensation,
As I fall into parts,
so pitiful; I become jejune,
Aren't we all in some slumber,
when we fall into asunder,
Disarmed and thrown,
into our hibernating cocoon,
Into one's fragments, we are shown,
events of the day,
That we relive at dusk,
as we walk through some scent
Of gorgeous musk,
we are someone else,
Where we meet outré,
to find in some mind's cage,
Some way out,
to asunder into some slumber.

Attraction of Solitude

Always, I have been alone
and through fate's generous handful
of others,
I have been the skin torn from the bone
and I know it's eternity—sure
enough beneath smiling covers,
Always, I have been one,
and through world's masses, clumsily
colliding to make two or three,
I have been the moon without the sun
and I know it's everlasting—sure
enough only my shadow I have always seen,
Always, I have been single
and through puzzle parties fitting together
to complete one's soul,
I have been the numbness, it's aftermath of tingle
and I know it's a perpetual course—sure
enough when I am buried so low,
Alone, for then, now and into the following
footsteps of the preying hours,
And their continual harassment,
and a bearable tomorrow,
For in my 18th year, it will become my most
favourable attraction.

Blank History

Throughout every season,
until the end of time,
I swirl my quill,
on paper lined.

When the lines are not there,
I shall know,
That I have passed on,
and let go of my bow.

I will write upon the blank,
and write my own history,
I will become a fragment,
and will in time become
Part of another's ancestry,
a faded memory.

I have seen oblivion,
it was when the skies parted ways,
Like the sea; I felt like Moses,
I led myself
Into the fear unknown, away,
and there was no month to replace
my passing of May.

The world had ended,
but only for I,
There was no more time,
o' needs must die.

O' no more I need,
I feel the ecstasy of rebirth,
None a body as extra baggage,
no bone hand thrusting through the earth.

Oh, it had been that I had died,
but remember upon blank,
I closed the final chapter,
and wrote my sincere good-bye . . .

"Good-bye."

Break Off With Despair

Swift, the
drift of despair,
Making us the bed of
Death, when we are
Not there,
o' but it is the torchbearer!
Bears my sadness with
loving care, sees me through
To an evening late,
'til I am pulling out
My breaking head's hair,
and a scalp that pains
Me,
the meld of that beautiful
Despair,
an undoubtedly reliable mate,
Never late,
always early, always there,
And a fleeting vision
contrives indecision,
Over what is fact and
what is ultimately fiction,
Maybe despair has to find
another soul,
Such low is no good,
and I shall tell it to *"go!"*

Cygnet Compassion

Young swans are indelible
upon the lake,
In Winter's evening hours
they make
The outline of a fictious
love heart,
Because long, slender necks
bend delicately not to make a star.

The lake is made indelible
with rose petal,
The cool Autumnal days
make a thousand golden medals,
Transform the place into
the Heavens
Because gold is not scattered
lightly, and peppered.

Swans float effortlessly upon
the brocade seas,
Made so with cyclamen floating
colours, shrouding the Hades,
Swans bow like corn
in Joseph's dreams . . .

Compassion for the dead, died in
the lake that keeps
Their souls like they keep their
dreams . . .

Death of a Clown

I drift through the play of life,
like Autumn's clothes
Blown about the air,
under surveillance of the atmosphere
Around me,
like oranges in the bowl,
Closely gazing into the pears,
or at least this is what I see,
Or at least this, above all, I fear,
oh, how things seem alive.

The play of life is enough to cringe at,
like bad comedy
In your eyes from the television,
or moments of humiliation that replay
Time and time again upon mind's screen,
enough to heed one over the edge of hope,
Where time seeps slowly from regret's incision,
the tearful clown I have been,
Hidden in my own special way,
oh, the one with Depression beneath one's hat.

The clown laughs to survive life's horror,
paints his face with absurdity
To complete his disguise,
and he laughs away his isolation
And tears of laughter blend with others,
like the deepest seas of blue that entwine
With the skies,
and he has brothers,
But they don't understand his jokes,
like a doctor who does not grasp
The essence or purpose of his patient,
but at the children's entertainment affair,
he will not be there for them tomorrow.

Deceived By All

They; an unctuously, fire-breathing
assemble,
Burns me too much with
a kind fire—it burns,
Acceptance—it is but urge
as all my gullibility trembles,
I paid for this error,
from potential companionship,
I—severed,
and retreat back in the lone wolf,
I am always likely to be.

Vernal traps of Spring,
they too; unctuously sneering
As I search for a beautiful something,
during what I can only recall
As a Winter's breathing,
that Spring dressed in hopeful apparel,
But loitering in their breath was
no succession of Christmas Carol,
T'was Winter for sure,
and looks in the time deceive me.

Denature It

Denature the soul,
worthless now
it's not our own,
Use it for the fireplace,
whenever we run short
on coal,
Throw it in,
pulling it out of our chests
like string,
For we have grown
worthless ourselves,
out of shape, out of place,
with skin so thin,
a walking waste.

And denature the ground,
so it will not hold
our weight in pounds.

Denature the water,
worthless now,
the ocean's distant daughter,
Use it to decorate the paths
of our sordid lives,
Liquid matter we won't be
able to keep once caught,
Let it sift out of the cracks
in our palms,
And roll down our useless
arms,
For it has become some sort
of vapour,

Not a survival to keep us here,
Starving, at loss, and all the while
that harmless air remains so calm,
For us it no longer reliably caters.

And denature the wine,
so it will not make of us,
Pathetic, self-absorbed mass
of swine through time.

Denature the pen,
worthless now,
scratching at some white,
Use it to make our cries for
help,
And when not in black and white,
who knows whether what we've
written is at all right,
Or whether it is a farcical affair,
by the dear in distress with the
long flaxen hair,
And no one is to blame but us,
we were not willing to lend,
before we changed our soul
for the worst,
And now everything we hold up
in the skies,
has become our foreground,
driven in that gloomy hearse.

And denature the books,
so that they will turn over themselves,
whenever we try to look.

And denature the Gods,
denature their generosity,
So we will become blasted unto
extinction,
from the world of which we made
of it—atrocity.

Depth

We wallow in depth,
no matter how light our step,
We hear some hospital chimes,
" . . . signifying what has died . . ."
Well, how were we to know,
that those chimes did hold,
Some ear-friendly hope,
some beige-speckled soap,
Of which to clean away the day,
and bring forth the moon's rays,
To bring to fruition the pretty
starry, streetlamp city,
We see everything so deep,
maybe that is why we so weep,
But a deepness must be relieved,
once in a while,
Out of life's enigma
that we desperately cleave,
And to us it shall reveal
that a yard is not a mile.

We wallow in depth,
no matter how light our step,
We see some lips,
and suppose it is some sinister wit,
Well, how were we to know,
that those dry lips did cradle from beneath,
some sincerity of Abel,
We see everything "under",
and break full into asunder.
And those lips did speak,
from ones only meek,
Of how life is yearly,
and a day is a week,

That time doth fly above our heads,
like the raven doth fly
to its resting bed,
"Of black-feather, surely . . .
he is a messenger for death,
To fly into our rooms at night,
and infiltrate the cleft,
That doth separate our dream from life,
and to become our minds,
Before in a deep slumber,
we lay dead, and have died,
Some foreseen death,
and taken some breaths,
Before we dined,
with the ghost,
And the ghost is our own,
and our body is woven,
with deepness and confusion . . ."

You see, I am deep, we are all . . .
And we answer the wolf's call,
with a fluttering of our arm wings,
And conclude that for if it is not our time,
that we were "seeing things",
Keeping a shotgun to our chest,
and sliding it under some duck feathered
pillow,
For fear the raven,
may perch upon our window sill,
And speak in mammal tongue,
different from our own,
And give us some wink,
before it has flown,

But truly from heart,
we do not fear the Death,
When we are as deep,
deep as one can get,
Down to one's grave,
while we are buried alive,
with wavering thoughts,
Ideations that are irrational to one's ear,
but to our own, 'tis a musical tune,
And it makes a world of sense,
like the simple of the dense,
Who are capable of that at least?
the black and white,
What is not to be questioned,
but I,
I find myself sequestered,
within a world of the deep,
And I will take a stroll into mind's depth,
before I let loose the weep,
And you see, I have rambled,
albeit, this is only a sample,
Of such the deep I hold,
and of which will grow old,
As will I,
but never too tired,
To look beyond a sky,
with a want to die.

Desert of their Age

The sands curl loosely
with every breath
of the sky,
And the elderly sift prudently
with fear enough of death
whilst the Sun begins to pry.

The light thrust down
upon experienced faces
in sweltering lack of draught,
And elderly in creased, old gown
with fear enough of spaces
because here, the present is past.

The past and present are one,
and the agonizing drone of time
will kill,
Time is the culprit—not the Sun,
and those elderly of all mind
Turn to face reality of their windowsills,
And shift so morosely into death
once their days are done.

Dignity Still of the Unfortunate Ill

Heavy weighed in the pinion
of illness,
He realised that there would
suffice a stillness,
To recoil at the manacles of rust,
of which his daily tears,
Had sent him upon the cusp,
of the revelation of recovery.

And he found in an argent
spoon,
His own features of which
fought at this doom,
In which he had perpetually
swooned!
That he was destined for
the grave,
But so there came,
his human look,
He had not lost face,
Through what evil had took!
Dignity still,
of the unfortunate ill!

Divide and Fear

Difference between the
elastic band and our
avaricious hands,
That elastic band embracing
every solid with a fear
there will be no tomorrow,
Like the terminally ill,
who resign to their sorrow,
The avaricious hands
embracing every flame with
a fear the fire will spread
like a ruthless cancer,
To burn away to ash will give us
our answer.

Difference between our
blind eye and our
avaricious eye,
That blind eye catching
the darkness with a fear
that it is the real world,
Like the real heights of life,
of which make bodies curl
in psychological vertigo,
The avaricious eye embracing
success with a fear that
without desire there is no drive,
To experience our fears,
we are fully alive.

Down Below

I wandered through the maelstrom,
of deadened, hapless gravestones,
This cigarette of mine,
stained with lipstick wine,
Stole colour from my lips,
and I took those gradual sips,
Of lingering, sweet scented breeze,
of which decorated the freeze,
Of bodies six-foot down,
even a cheerful, jovial clown,
Lay down there in the silence,
of cold and sheltered ambience,
The victims of the Grim,
had taken her and him,
To a palace amongst the clouded
atlas maps,
As God's angels proceed their
heavenly wraps,
Around their fresh-born dead
souls,
and add a pang of warmth to their
bodies cold.

Drag Exterior

O' burn to ash my cigarette city,
tobacco built with paper coating,
Construction of places
burns inside of me,
O' is it not pretty,
those drags I take,
So as not to believe
addiction a Devil makes!

Burn to ash my chapel,
and a Mary,
And those realistic constructions
of stone and bricks,
At least made of ash,
they are lapidary,
In hue of Stone Age greys,
of a fine ash silk.

Or truncate my cigarette,
midway through its cremation,
And make of it,
some dazzling creation,
Let the ash burn into my hands,
Give me the dust and thought,
to build some new land,
From these wrinkled, yellow
hands,
O' I know the parable well,
a wise man doth not build
his house upon the sands.

But I can build my city
upon ash and dust,
The smoke I thrust
into my throat,
My principles are built upon
contemplation and trust,
And I put every faith in that
slender cylinder ,
With a white and orange coat,
and on such dream-fuelled smoke,
I shall never choke,
Only upon my dream,
if I were to regurgitate it,
It will seem I will die,
before my friend is lit.

During Some Storm

I disclose to you,
of how a ferocious
tempest wet the terrain,
And a precipitating roof to clothe
us drenched,
Let us all at once, refrain
from our enthusiastic errands,
Nevertheless, our pores were quenched,
with abundant water in their gallons,
And I do not lie, when I say
they were crying out of their
tiny mouths and begging,
Beneath frilled shirt and suffocating legging,
for such teeming, tepid rain.

Pithy, closed umbrellas,
albeit, drawn out use thereafter,
And the ground wells up, a
crying flatland,
And all essence of pathos has
been captured,
Saturated, sycophant boots,
licking the ground's thin layer of tears,
And one foot unto another, recruits
though in unavoidable debt of arrears,
to the ground's sorrow,
For its sadness it borrows
for gratification,
For a glossy, glamorized skin,
it's earned through yards of
human vacation,
All about this flood land
town.

Enemy to Art: A Simpleton's Life Lesson

A simpleton, I will announce,
listened to Bach and Mozart
and Strauss,
But little did inspire his
clockwork brain,
Through, through the minute,
and starting again.

When a maverick's clock
ticks by,
The minutes are delayed
by each thoughtful sigh,
And he gives birth to new thought,
as the ticks will die,
he is a master of his time.

But with a Simpleton
sitting at an empty desk,
A safe life lived
to sacrifice his best,
As idleness progresses forward,
and production moves West,
And so is gone, his very best.

He did not look beyond
the sky,
To question each star with
thinning eyes,
He did not put a pen to parchment,
to question what?
The symbols dark had sent.
And little did inspire

his clockwork toy,
That wondrous thing
that basks in the skull,
That of which, inside
this unseen platform,
Of which we live and die
a thousand times,
and a thousand times more!

He did not see the
secretive soul,
Beneath Man's disguise
so thick and bold,
He did not put a
paint to brush,
To create the impression
that makes and destructs—
life's own lesson.

His lesson must be learnt
past the repetitive ticking,
Is that life must delay
and forward the process of thinking,
Life must be drank
through the dews morning air,
Our money be earned before
it can be banked,
And that life may be tough,
but in the end, proves fair,
Life must be learnt through
brush, look and pen,
The piece de resistance

of ten thousand men,
and ten thousand men more!
His lesson must be taught
by the artists of the earth,
To wipe clean his life's slate
of lifeless dirt,
With the dirt of controversy
to stain his mind,
To develop into one whose
intentions are revolutionary kind,
Through brush, look, pen of blues.

Euphoria

Euphoria—
a fire dances,
Dancing decorum
beneath the mantel,
Beyond the cold
is a warming gesture,
The only answer . . .
to all our cool, rigid
prayers,
Fire dances in
EUPHORIA . . .
It's alive and living
in some same old
story of Winter.

Euphoria—
a cool wind swirls, and squirms—
Cooler than our sorrow prayers—
through that fire—no concern
For now chilled skin through to bone,
and there is no absence of relent on
Atmospheric breath of night—its song
of suffer and eventual sleep
Of which none shall wake . . .

Cool wind swirls, and squirms in
EUPHORIA—
It's alive and living
in some same old story of Winter.

Ex Cathedra

From the chair, I abdicated,
t'was the chair of bareness
and fact,
Slowly sinking into someone's
created carpet trough below the fairness
of hand-held tract.

Fair, in that
contents of the tract
Told of a dying man's pact
with death,
And with diminishing breath,
I prepared and wept,
For I became involved with the tale.

I gradually lowered my feet
forth into the carpet trough,
And perpetually sank, a
dangerous seat
Of despair, and off
with my head,
I am too close to the dead,
and from the chair . . .
Morbidity is my anchor.

Experience vs. Death:
An Old Man's suffering

An old man told me
he'd seen everything;
Said he knows the
human—
That he knows everyone,
knows how to fire
And to hold a gun,
knows how we work
For a pittance;
Money is worth
as much as you,
And we will die
eventually,
So it's not worth the
wonder of immortality,
(it's hardly worth enough).
Said he knows the soul
like the routes he took
To get to work; like a mole
on his now drooping arm,
(gravity is fighting his youth
for domination)
And he willingly gained all
knowledge from the book,
But all past fears
become excruciating reality,
The betrayal of a
kiss upon the cheek,
That betrayal cruelly smears
all over
To make of him painful, twisted vanity,
And well . . .

that loss upon the horses,
That careless bet . . .
it returned with blood-
stained slip,
No remorse—
nature
Included in this—
humanity
Must run, walk, crawl
its course,
Surely he must know that,
that in dying,
Limping slowly in agonizing,
irreversible fear,
Eaten, humiliated
and mauled
By his living days,
and the past condenses into
The same liquid substance
as the present,
And he sits opposite me,
clawing an already
Tattered chair
(gave him a head start),
The liquid macerates
his skin,
Bringing ugly friction
to fruition,
Drowns his pitiful, thinning
hair,
(It's given up the fight),
" . . . and so have I,"
He read my eyes
like a knowledge book-

The entrance to thought,
and then he feebly died,
Look what the Death had
finally caught—
An experienced old man,
and my half-biased modern
age rant!

I rant no more,
and now my own body
Is beginning to pour
into the basket of my chair . . .
I am drowning amidst the
gyration of times gone by,
Filled with inescapable
reminiscence,
And I have no resistance,
against that harsh old memory!

I am not likely to get out
of it.

Fears of the Dead

I dread I cannot quell,
I fear I cannot
perforate the ceiling,
To enable the sky to pour
through; upon my head,
And if I am weary,
if I lack happy feelings,
it is I that am dead,

If I dread some light,
I am still very sensitive,
I will still inhabit
the dark corners of rooms,
Like the black clouds that loom
over my head,
And in life,
it is I that am dead.

I do not want a flame
of light,
To set me alight,
when I do not warm
To a fire's friendliness,
too much, too close,
It spurns lively growth!
And I am no more!
Do not make me soar!
I do not believe in flying!
My heart is done with dying!
Leave me silent in obduracy

Finding Common Ground

How the Sun of Absolutism
scorched brick red; that
feverish glow,
The time of a golden brute to
slam his drum,
Unleashing hot rays upon
the land below.

O' how feeble it doth shine,
when composer almighty God
commanded it not beat,
Its power it doth
mechanically bind;
The walk; stiffness of
what were yesterday—dancing feet.

How we train ourselves to
file away our pain in
draws marked "x",
Consolation—we feel the same,
or maybe we do not
as layers of flesh from past delirium
perish and rot.

How no one will hear our tale
nor hear our name,
And by God, the Sun wept
and showered upon me . . .
never-ending rain!

Fish' Fate

He watches his family eat,
ruthless barbarians,
The majority are the elite,
and on the plate,
What was plucked from
the gigantic aquarium,
No sympathy; revolt, they ate,
as time—posthumously for
Those dead cut creatures
went on, and on . . .

Augment humanity with
nutritional values,
Au revoir to the animal,
it's nutritional apparel
It wears like any man
that wears his cravat
like a noose,
They know the ceremony,
squirming, agonizing, beneath
Glittering stars, as men sat
hungrily in boats, upon mounts,
As the vegetarian wearily counts
the days 'til the ban is due.

"We've got enough!"
As the vegetarian takes a
fisherman by the scruff.

For The Best, Remain Children

Everywhere is inhabited by
a child,
We are constantly in search of
the new
In our minds,
and we will never grow up
And flower,
We are in too much of need
of every power,
Our ambitions—designed
by the wild
Inner being,
and we extract from it
Some fleeting
notion; fast-paced motion,
The fruitful tree in
the deserted orchard,
Maybe it is for the best,
our befallen crest
Of what was once
social stability.

Ghost of the Banshee

I lay on such an elegant
flower,
Like no other;
too strong—it held its body
as if it were its brother,
Whole lot of droplets thrashing
upon that tear-shaped skin,
It could hold the world,
bear it like a gift,
Something
wonderful,
Something
heard,
It represented me,
I am the dead,
I am the risen,
I am the banshee,
foretold death inside
this prison,
They call it "earth"
but I can see death,
Before it occurs,
I call this wisdom.

August flowers that retain
their statue when I find
some other,
Let mine own stand tall,
amongst its brothers,
O', how the rest hang limply
beneath earth's nightly covers,
They call it "sky",
I call it trouble,
Once it collapsed upon me,

None could save me,
the luck of a four-leaf clover
could not have stopped it,
There is no prevention,
they call it "death",
To release one's life,
up to the Heaven's,
Prevents us from carrying on,
well, death is prevention,
Prevents our voice—frail,
from telling the saddening dirge
of our latter days,
What is worse?
To have carried on
in grey, aging song,
To prolong such a bygone
tale until all Heavens break!

Well, all those other flowers . . .
I rip them all I may find,
Cadence of "tsh . . ." with
sorrow in mind,
Attached to some child-like
ways,
Some overtone of identity,
for I am the wailing banshee,
The flowers are person,
there are to be deaths
around the place,
'Cept this flower here,
this is mine—
I am it,
I have already died,
I swore I felt above the clouds,

I surpassed them when all
skies broke,
There were no sounds
through what death took,
And there was no banshee
to signal my passing of March,
O' they are as such—
that before me, there were none,
I was the first,
In second life, with gift
I was touched,
Before people were population,
then when they were sparsely
scattered,
O' they did not pray to their lost,
none to lose,
None they have lost,
of birth—no bruise,
No limit reduced,
make mistake,
And learn the truth,
and I have already died.

Re-growth of every petal,
rumour has it,
I was not always so . . .
the banshee,
I had to die to become heroine,
O' what's God's game,
He plays it so carelessly!
What world am I left in,
torn brocade of my once blue skies!

Glass

Timeless; immune to the tragedy
of aging,
Immune to water,
but not to the fist,
Real eager ones out there,
and so, perchance, I ought to . . .
If all keen, violent ages of fist, persist,
remove all windows,
Will it prevent the fist owners'
stares?

To prevent what potential can often
do . . .
If the owner is no coward for
running, red rivers decorating hands
And staining clothes a scarlet,
eliminate provoking protection—
An act of "early prevention" to not be
born a war!

To drain the bodies of water
of water,
The fisherman relishes in witnessing
the fish alive,
"No pain, no gain!"
must break his heart,
As before the start,
his heart was a locket full . . .

And so without the water,
he must not ought to
retrieve his fish—
they're dead,
Cease to squirm, wriggle,
they are a little
Bereft of any will . . .

And what will a fisherman
do,
That does not include
drinking the wine
From its container,
without removing the cork,
He must abandon lest
he should chew
A meal so undeserved,
he will resume his walk
And what he had not caught
will leave him a better man,
Saner,
that "potential" could not do!

What the fisherman had learnt:
" . . . *that darkest potential,*
when denied through disarm,
When heat cannot die
through open window,
from coal burnt blacker,
And when some animals escape
slaughter,
With absence of farms
and barriers . . ."

". . . And when my windows
do not exist,
fists—
they find not human face
but pure air . . .
And the fisherman will find
them there,
miles away,
The energy used for a
better something,
Upon ground and burnt, old cirrus
amidst the bass drum of the Sun,
The anger, thuggery and slacking
are there,
And are there
to stay . . ."

Heaven's Palominos

The prairie peppered with
peregrinating palominos,
In circular motion these
white tails of authority go,
Snowy manes and
darkened eyes,
Taking those acres of luscious
emerald by surprise,
With grace in stepping,
acres indebted,
To a horse's gold,
upon it's back,

The air that hold
the beauty we lack,
Perchance, it's Heaven's,
the Devil's horse is a six,
But alas! God's is a seven,
and triumph he shall,
With his golden riches
bestowed on earth,
Of a beautiful animal,
the ground it burns,
With love and a Heavenly
touch,
Hitherto, our eyes often
demand to much,
And we are not beautiful,
or Heavenly as such,
Not like a horse,
run our fingers through it's
hair,
Unlike ourselves, so coarse,
with all that armour we wear.

His Midnight Eye

He had lost that glimmering
crescent of his eye,
The colour dimmer in
his midnight eye,
O' vigilant sage of nocturne
in the pupil of his eye,
How his mind taught
it thorough,
The observation that must gather
in his midnight eye,
All senses; touch, smell, a ear
will abidingly and electronically
cover, for
What is the
sight and his identical brother,
Lips will shrivel,
and utter not a word,
Nostrils will stay unphased,
fingers will dither
On in lazy malaise
cracking—showing
Its anger days,
and all the while,
Pictures will slither,
into that midnight eye,
The heavily populated world,
in his midnight eye.

Holding Hands with the Night

I stare into the heart of the stars,
and their presence beats,
From a distance far,
Where the dead stroll along the
cloud's ebbs and
Of where in awe of the sky,
Eyes and sky meet.

I inhale the night's breath deep
into a state of long forgotten daze,
On a patch of grass from where I take
the leap,
Where I live and die a thousand times
in the eye of God and
Of where in awe of the night,
I fix upon the darkness
my bloodshot gaze.

I caress the breath,
lest I should lose my soul,
The hot pang of shivering death
confirms I'm here
vertical upon grass' horizontal
outstretched corpse and
Of where in awe of my presence,
once the Sun emerges over the
Plain, aged hills,
I shall lay old,

I shall grow cold,
Perchance, I'll go,
For a Sun, it has potential enough
with it's hot, block stare,
To take from me my dignity,
and confirms one's fear,
That one is still holding hands with the night,
and one should,
In Sun's imposing rays,
not be there.

Homeless Folk

Oh, how the homeless
are scattered in sides of streets,
Oh, how to them—the cities and towns
are coastless,
How dying in the raw, sharp
cold—this, hard to beat,
In terms of poverty.

Oh, how the poor
are peppered under shops' canopies,
Oh, what qualifications have they—
we cannot be sure,
Pushed a wreck in front of
our public eye—they think it insanity,
In terms of what is supposed to be.

Oh, how the pitiful
are given nameless graves on the floor,
Oh, temporary to become permanent—
dead, dying, gone amongst the city full,
A few pounds to prolong the death,
and save it for another day.

Home Soil

The grass is dead and yellow,
the flowers are also dead,
The wind is but an echo,
the grey ground in grey dread,
For what will happen next,
a sense of deep regret,
For being here beneath,
an air so damp and wet,
The wind in self-pitying cry,
for what will follow suit,
A deadened wave of salute,
for the leaves of trees that die,
Moving them along,
in a howling dirge of saddened pursuit,
And the flowers' corpse exists,
for what will carry on,
A creation in dreadful song,
for its body in gruesome twist,
Moving to and fro',
in the soil where all belong.
And the grass' deceased old hue,
for what will continue to be,
Death for dying flowers to see,
albeit, it's nothing new,
They've seen it all before,
in dying they don't feel,
A sense of grieving, so,
a deadened, stoic shield.

Hypochondriacs

They squander their souls
upon the rocks and stones,
Quite hot like a thousand
suns
In the cold,
marked by desperation,
And of it—
not woes.

Girls and boys who'd sworn
they'd undoubtedly saw
The Devil in predictable
attire with sharpest horns,
And that since the days of being born,
they had ever long suffered such hardship
of a thousand wars.

But they will not divulge to
me in confession,
That a thousand wars in reality
was none,
And that their presence shines
like a single sun . . .
And that deceit and compulsive lie fire
like a loaded gun . . .

When will they run . . .
out of the bullets,
That sustains their awareness
with empathetic ones . . . ?

I Do Not Hate "the Blues"

I do not hate the blues,
like a Narcissist does not loathe
himself,
For I become those darkest hues
of blue,
I cannot possibly lose,
for all other possibilities—
I am no longer deep-footed in the
wealth
Of concrete cast light by the Sun,
o', "the Blues"—
I am a reflection,
and I am you,
So I do not hate,
when Devil commands
And sets all controls of
the soft computer,
Like the wet sands,
Devil built a fortress,
Built one route, and
I am obliged, in trance to walk it,
And exist in the blue,
to drown in the ocean,
O', "the Blues"—
I will always be you!

Infatuation Vanity Affair

Yonder upon the shattered
portrait in motion,
It moves as I wish,
its life-long promotion,
Reflecting of me
something garish!

Its frontier of darkened
steel,
I, estranged inside,
but the mirror does not
feel,
The essence of me that
died!

Scattered upon the floor
of carpet black,
Frozen fish still, in
the oil-polluted sea,
Silvery transparency
I so lack,
when it does not reflect
of me!

Peroration with this
shattered mirage,
A mirror copying my
faces' cracks,
A broken, petty visage,
Though it means the world
to purified glass!

The glass and I—
we are united,
A couple of solitudes
occupying one space,
A single solitude sighted,
in my reflected,
pernicious face!

A mockery of one
every night and day,
Every time I occupy
the sheltered life,
Every time I try to play
life's pernicious rules,
For all I am, a shattered
housewife!

Inflicted Desires

We inflict upon ourselves
desires,
To be within reach, of arm's
length, the remote control to its
puppet electronic device,
We become the liars,
striving to see a double of six on
the oblong faces of dice,
It's our desire—
that it could have been,
To have had a yearning for years
of unblemished joy, like the
Uncontaminated water that unleash
from our homes' taps, we have
seen,
But to put our desires to the wrong
purpose, of us we reveal the beast,
And I cannot say what is
undoubtedly immoral or the
Polarity of that,
but when we are controlled by
Self infliction of desires,
where are we at . . . ?

It Was Home

Moss stalks up lapidary brick
like clematis,
Climbing toward the Heavens
with colourful offering,
Though this growth is a
dirty green,
Telling of tenants lives in
the gutter,
Cenotaph drainpipes,
cerise lips crying,
At the drainpipes,
derived from the eye's watering waste,
Water the flower lips
with salt tears,
To spurn sorrow's growth,
and sadness laughter,
Beneath this colossal canopy,
a derelict construction,
What once was home,
bereft of life,
Bereft of families' fruit,
once ready and ripe,
Ready to be taken,
in what once was such a
Home grown life,
and rest my own weary bones,
Beside the bones of my wife,
whilst the cold contaminates the air,
And it cuts through the living,
like some carving knife,
This is life,
this is life.

Junky

"Hit me up" with heroin,
"Fix me" a line of cocaine,
Let me into the gates of ecstasy,
all aboard the Delirium Train,
Not in need of underlying tracks
of family empathy,
Present me with Valium,
deal me some marijuana,
Induct me into chemical-induced
elation,
To fall from disgrace in front of
my mother and father,
Thereafter leave them in fear at
the Cocaine Station,
I see black smoke infested
compartments,
Weeping eyes and bloodshot
faces,
Let me out of the Cocaine Train,
allow me to take care of all the
desolate spaces inside my head,
Put a picture back inside its frame,
I don't want to be killed by death!

But a morning I cannot feel,
"Fix me" a line of amphetamine,
Let me into the gates of adrenaline,
take my bloodless specimen,
Full of us addicts' illegal, self-satisfying
penicillin,
But in economic peril,
present me with the "Hand of God",
Resting upon my eyes' skin wall,

To enable me to see everything
so colourfully warped and extremely
odd,
To accompany a miniature green
swordsman ; the voice within that calls them,
Love me in this comatose
paradise of hope,
And talk to Frank,
by God, he knows,
Of narcotic stupor and an
administered amount of dope,
How acid poisons my mental assurance,
'til I'm left with no endurance
for life's sobriety,
Let me die.

Lady of the Sea

She floats upon the water,
like a message in a bottle,
Mottled like the sky at
night, marked with stars,
Tars the sea with human
curves,
Concaving like the fearful
in agonising curl,
Knees reaching their lips
within their psychological pool of whirl,
Her topaz fins create fury
within the sea of calm,
Her language, unearthly, chants
like a Heavenly psalm,
Her stretch of hair—a fine shade of teal,
ties us in emotion; though she cannot feel,
The feelings she spurns in others,
of life-long companionship and dream-phased lovers,
Her loss of sentience,
compensated by liaisons
With the rough of the tides,
she makes of them feathers,
Spinning to the ground,
in their gradual stride,
The euphony dispersed from
her swollen lips two,
Evinces her content of brackish
water; an electric hue,
She teeters like the cyclists
embarking upon the new,
And she reveals the insecurities
inside of you,

But with such grace through
unsteady existence,
She fills us up with beauty
in an instance,
All sense of time lost in
a sea's great tranquillity,
To abstain from the life of
the town, and inhabit this vicinity,
O', but we are not,
but the mermaid is,
Although on looking, we have forgotten
our definitive sadness!

Let it Commence

We can make a war this morning,
we can carry it on to evening late,
And war we are always born in,
when we are thrown into the narrow and straight,
Because of this, we indulge in protest,
war is always there,
And life is obviously no test,
when it is morally right and fair,
And we can make some peace for now,
but we cannot carry it forward,
We make a class of children bow
to teachers—but this is no good,
Children are soldiers from onset,
and peace will turn to war,
We are good in where there is debt,
and will act out peace no more,
There will be nothing left,
supple skin left rough and sore,
And maybe some good will be kept,
But we will use it all for war.

Life's Darkest Veil

Gigantic clouds are with me in the day,
and when the dark veil of
morose,
Paints them away,
the veil is so close,
to life's mattress upon which I weakly lay.

There are no starry whites,
when the dark veil of
deplorable,
Paint them out of
my gigantic life canvas,
Of which is despairingly soft
to touch,
To crush and break,
the vulnerability is made.

And my heavy heart cannot carry
its weight,
With the world's weight and
I,
It will surely break,
and bleed no more, blood no more,
Let my spirit soar,
to the Heavens high,
And release me from indissoluble
night,
That acquaints itself with I,
even through day's loving light.

Where the clouds are all white,
and a place I cannot sink,
For in that glorified kingdom,
I do not have to think,
Nor give sorrow my name,
nor come unprepared for
a heart in some hand's grasp,
That show me I no longer feel.

And that I and the grey clouds
are one and the same,
And that in this kingdom
I do not have to plead nor politely ask,
For Death and its friends,
for I have already been
A ear for life's rough, intimidating
rasp,
And now I suffer like
flowers in a gentle breeze,
Yes, no more,
for this heavenly kingdom,
I carry its keys,
in my fresh-born hands,
And I life I once knew,
stretches a distance far,
like the sands.

Like The Seasons

The young man followed the
burning sun,
And followed it still once
day was done,
He clambered up the
highest tree,
He could not reach, yet
he could see,
The crescent of foil in
suspense of the sky,
Why not the sun he
wondered why,
The moon in all its
silvery splendour,
A ghastly night it
could not mend, or
Drown the world
with angelic light,
The young man sought
immortality of the rays,
To protect the world from
a midnight malaise!
He was the type to hunt
down Death,
To stand his ground with
hungry breath,
And once the nightfall
vanished and left,

He felt he was the
saviour of light,
But he saw no sun,
no sphere so bright,
Not so much a
saviour as such,
But a martyr of
greed,
Bitten off more than
a hand could feed.

Masters of Ceremony

Through the hue and cry
Of Euthanasia,
Through the sharpness
Of that colossal razor,
Through the predator's pounce,
Of the malkin,
Through that alley
Of conditions dank and dim,
Through the masks
Of Plaster Paris, ashen,
Through the augury
Of the assassin,

Through all such events
Of what is infinitely bad,
The gift is in the right to die,
When eyes and the
Times cry,
The gift is in the harm,
When our existence is carved,
The gift is in the hunting pet,
A token gesture of its debt,
The gift is in the places of damp,
Where there is rejuvenation
Waiting for man,
The gift is in the colour that
Drains and dies,
By no means "pale" in
Rembrandt eyes,
And the gift is in the omen,
For if not, the preparation
Lays dormant.

Of those properties six,
For if we had the audacity
To mix:
And so, through the sharpness
Of the assassin,
All of our worlds would
Plummet, crashing,
Endless Terror!
We are all Masters of Ceremony.

My Descent into Hell

I

Stood in light's absence,
I prized open the ancient
pocket watch,
And the exact present was
not captured,
All sense of time had been
shot,
Into the hot sun of oblivion,
and I was at once fearful,
This atmosphere so evil
as the Pharaoh that kills
every boy young,
And this destitution of my
soul,
Nearing full
of Satan's anguish orchestra,
The screaming violins of
murder,
And Jezebel, I swore I heard
her,
I began to demonstrate sins,
I felt them inside of myself,
like a wet needle scraping my
inner being,
And I endured all of this by
myself,
And of only a pitch blackness
I was seeing.

II

I became the time,
and decided that it was fair,
That I waded through sprawled
out barks on my level,
But in darkness; like this, there
was no shine,
To turn a jewel,
and discover it was simply dark
purple,
And my tousled, hanging hair
resembled that of my soul in
strips,
A wind so dominating,
it blew them about so forcefully,
And inserted through the voids
in my lips,
To make of me anti-life,
in a place that was not
accommodating,
And I cannot find that path
of light,
Made so by sprinkling of
rays,
The dark cradled in my sight,
with a touch of darkest grey.

III

Oh, it felt like years,
isolated in deepest fear,
Oh, I fear for my life,
its pleas that none will hear,
The distance so far,
too far to reach a single ear,
And so sudden, the ground
became fire,
Did I pass for a cursed one?
Did acceptance into Hell
take years,
Has a life before this
expired,
Has Hell, for me, begun?
But I plead, I did not consent,
to this bleakest of all places,
And now emerging faces,
from out beneath the spaces,
All heavy skin, and bone
structures,
All features painfully thin,
is this the place for us,
When we are all guilt-ridden
with Sin,
And I dread to think,
though I am on the brink,
of becoming just like them.

IV

They did not speak to me,
all I heard was sighs,
Under the auspices of
that man with horns,
Who destroyed what I knew
of the skies,
And made of me austere born,
for I was afraid to step some
steps further,
Toward the deadened end,
and I, built up with fervour,
In this hellish, demon of events,
Sought a place by the fire,
but the closest I could get,
Was to stand on this woodland
vast funeral pyre,
Where flames did not leave
burning scars,

Did not brand me a burned
victim of heat,
But of my soul, it did mar,
And of life, I was obsolete,
My God, where is the line,
to cross with huge relief,
Where is the soul of mine
to protect and rightfully keep?
No, what once was my own,
has become the Devil's gift,
From my God I am disowned,
And such heavy soul that
no faith can lift.

V

I took role in such hideous play,
directed by the blistered hand,
Made so with the sin of jealousy,
cast off from God's own land,
But here, I am to stay,
for he will not turn face away,
From my piteous state,
I am part of his hideous ways,
I admit, I committed heresy,
in God's sharpest eye,
For I named myself a God,
and a disgusting being I died,
Only to fall from earth,
and land unto the care of evil,
In abundance, he'll cast his iron,
over my weeping brow,
Like Saul who was fed to
lions,
And the difference to consider,
that God had saved him, and
how,
I have no one to save me here,
and alone, I mutter and shiver,
And I am resigned to this for now
and forever,
And when the earth shall shatter
into a trillion pieces,
Well, it will not matter,
my agony will not cease,
I damned here for eternity long,
and instruments of that thing
pain,

Will drone on in pitiful song,
and never will it stop,
It will carry on,
thereafter and forever more.

VI

A place in Hell does not teach
me,
Nor does it preach,
those words of God,
To live by and to keep,
and here in my descent's
garden,
I frown and weep,
and nothing can assuage
the pain and grief,
And I am no longer ardent
for the life I carry,
I am a slave to the cardinal
of horror and sorrow,
And I have been married
to the day of which none more
shall follow,
This everlasting dirge of a day
in eternal regret,
No happiness or outlet,
to fill what is hollow,
And what is hollow,
is my body and mind,
And of the life I once knew
it is for that I crave and pine,
And now I shall seek a place
to lie,

And at every second, I
shall perish and die,
In the eyes of Satan,
oh, it's approaching late,
and I'm leaping into the
fiery sky below my feet,
My world has been turned
upside down,
And there is no solace,
nor hope for me now.

Necropolis of Melancholy

In the Necropolis of Melancholy,
revenant shades sway through
the trees' breath
'Erelong the bell shall thunderously
chime,
Albeit, the silence will be kept.

In the Necropolis of Melancholy,
past poets of pale pallor,
Shuffle through the trees' breath,
dictators limply shouldered,
albeit, the lost and fallow.

In the Necropolis of Melancholy,
past kings of ugly grimace,
Besiege the eroded stones,
erasing at the grey,
to find a way back home.

No Sun, Just Oblivion

I know not what bullies
the moon at night—
His day; his dawn,
I only know from where
he obtains his refreshing light,
Of which is out-done by
his dealer, by the morn.

But supposing the moon
takes a Sun's light,
and does not give it back . . .
What he doth owe from night,
not to be amused, the Sun!
This is Oblivion.

Oh, Sharp Memory!

Old side streets glitter with menacing past memory
like sky's gentle stars,
Though no gentle impression creeps upon mind and shoulders,
and recollections make stone of heart,
Tars it lapidary, make full fit the side streets; a recurrent,
sharpened cemetery . . .

Does not glaze with softness, one's barely opened saddened,
glassy eye,
And nothing inside that cosmos or mine will hone one's
eyes like the disguise
Sky has behind the softest breadth of cirrus; those candid
side streets; fiercely sharp as the sky is maddened . . .

By the brightness of the fierce Sun that controls the days
of our lives like hearts control our destinies,
For memory makes sharp, cold bitterness of despairingly
lenient softness, oh where art thou terrestrial
entities to build my cosmos; that June or May's mark one
year before would not be set in its awful ways?

That old side streets would not glitter at all of past
like the fiercely, irreversible Sun's light
Upon a crescent shape half-bitten by its own jealousy—
that it makes glitter of the night when Sun dies,
Spites itself on numerous ends of Day, when Sun perishes fast—
oh, everything but memory does not last!

Does it not last,
we all born from crematory ashes of our brothers
And sisters,
this sharpened, dominant cemetery!
Old flames, and smooth paper present,
burns to ashes our bones,
Let us collapse, devoid of spine, in anguish!
The cemetery, of sharpest memory, has us within
its immortal claws, again!

Pity Those Trees

Trees remain oscillate,
bowing, recoiling,
in agony separate.

Perchance,
they are undecided,
in rooted stance.

Surveying us is all seasons,
yet they shiver,
In Winter's breeze,
all year round.

Perchance,
they are rooted from a ground of anxiety,
And suffer fantastic,
in the nature of piety.

And they lose their fruits in
January,
In a grieving orchard,
rub in the salt,
In their frozen bark's gauges,
who would suspect they have died,
From such colossal grief,
spreading from the inside.

Rebellion

Curtains are aged and well
used during the world's dark
Blanket concealing life
behind closed doors,
And we are hushed to sleep by
the saddening trees,
And Nocturne's whispering breeze—
nothing less,
nothing more,
How young ones temporarily die
with considerable ease,
Beneath the shining pride
of moonlight—
Nocturne's own, belittling disease,
And curtains drape in piteous,
idle ways,
That they have most certainly
learnt
From a child's idle gaze,
and they do not flutter in
Dead of night,
but yet still, they clutter the life
of the night lover's might,
To step out a d exist in after hours'
shield,
Against all promise that we'd not show
it how we yield,
Feeble, yet still . . .
a feast for one's own sky,
Feast hastily without caution,
lest in bed's own blankets,
We shall wither . . .
and die.

Restless Agony

I lay in semi-darkness,
those moments that do
Mark us
Restless, poor souls!

I sat in bed, and upright,
To wage a war of some flight,
To write and
Full of vague hope
Of that of what I had wrote
Would become the perfect
Anecdote,
But ate such words 'til
I choked.

The Four Seasons of Vivaldi,
Would become the soft
And sandy
Seaside of my wishes,
But were blown about
To wreckage!

And so, to no avail,
This perennial, durable tale,
This unyielding, restless state,
Of which, I, wholly awake,
Would drag on to
The morning late, and
Yes, I did resign,
I was the sleepless bait!

Yonder on that staircase,
Of my tired, hopeless face,
The sleepless sight exploited,
There is no rest for solace!

Sorrow's Room

In the bare room left
with nothing,
Unfurnished and bare
like the rooms in my
Head, I am suffering
like the laying sick
In their beds,
and a door closed to
Me, open to presents from Sorrow,
the presence of emptiness
Like the yawning hole of my
heart, I am borrowing
The Sun's light before
darkness sets me apart,
And before shadows are
cast, to show I'm there
But In life I am here
like the agonising day of my
Night, I am spared
the participation as
Depression holds me tight,
and I am eternity's walls in
Sorrow's Room.

Stanzas (Written to the night)

I raised my chin profusely,
when night was silently dead,
Toward the upper atmosphere,
where dark and light were paired,
As moon had cast a sphere,
It's glowing, hazy circumference,
I watched from afar with gravity,
as it lost the fullest of clarities.

The moon made an appearance,
to sleep above public watch,
And scattered randomly and sparsely,
were illuminated, shying dots,
Awaiting the performing starlings,
by which time, the dots—no more,
And I watched from afar with fear,
as spread-winged owls began to cheer!

The trees began to sway,
complimentary to the winds of plangent,
From afar, the reprised wolf,
It's deep cries signalling the danger,
In other than the rough of the bull,
but of the hills that do bear eyes,
And as I watched from afar with fright,
two eyes did emerge from the night!

As madness of the time crept upon me,
I felt my pulse like no other,
Racing toward some attack,
with this heart inside of another,
My sight became of that outside some Cadillac,
peering through tinted windows without success,
Now this horrid phantasmagoria,
of such deep, unsettling aura!

Maybe the time will confirm one's fear,
that the night is here to stay,
And of all that I hold so dear,
will become stranded in the fearless day!

Starvation Lands: Waiting on the Captain

Marooned upon the starvation sands,
hallowed be the flag,
hallowed be the captain,
The time roughly drags
in flush to reach the place
Where sea and land link
and banish, make good
fill of the space,
Link like doomed newly weds,
unknowingly tied for a lifetime
in pretty, strong lace,
Endurable,
living upon starvation lands,
Endurable—
it is the only way,
Endurable,
and the man devoid of religion heart
has for days, issued forth the word of God;
He prays,
plays the game of faith,
Whether or not he truly believes,
he is waiting on the captain.

But the torn halyard broke,
torn again, but for the final time,
And his suffering skin is all
wrapped in
Thick sadism of the air that
stood still,
Will and forever more;
through all seasons and never
had one saw . . .
such wannest of all men,

Will and forever more . . .
we will see his eyes again,
Even they do not bring forth
the seas,
This land is water-less,
to morph; the metamorphosis,
Power to bring ten thousand men
to their living peril,
And bring out of a man
all seven . . .
deadliest sins a Devil made!

The captain has retreated
to the lighthouse,
That falsest of marooned Man's
hopes,
This heart-breaking of all
facades!

Stream of Consciousness: Take One

I listen to "my" music the modern way,
well, it's not "my" music,
I didn't make it in the past nor today,
and music melds beautifully with the images
upon the screen like angels in the Heavens'
airy abode,

I didn't have a clue, I didn't know
why the character bent on death,
Bent over the forest-green bars, and in
no time at all, was a mangled two dimensional
piece of Death,
And my breath is visible like the trees outside,
driving themselves at the future from the two-bedroom
flat,

Television's music dictates everything I see,
until I bring to a halt the hearable volume,
And from the corner of my eye, a bird on the outside
fleets upward,
Birds want to reach the Heavens,
Because humans are as hungry,
as the Devil is contented . . .
Like a human sets his or herself on fire
and enters
Heaven before their murderer does.

My head throbs like the heart that seldom does not,
and what have I got to my existence,
Other than the throbbing head upon broad shoulders,
Every second, every present that falls behind,
I am progressing older,
Confessing my current interpretations and activities
and thought upon this piece of technology . . .

To express my insight, however trivial . . .
from this,
It does not get any better,
like the wounded, to be fatal,
Whose relatives discuss the funeral arrangements
at their side,
Abide by suffering, abide by the Devil and
you will wound his power like the knife lodged
In the heart of you,
Take careful steps toward the Heavens,
and disappoint the deathly, cunning Devil.

Television Lies

I see the accident-prone sort
reaping the benefit,
From their well-thought deficit,
of felon not caught,
They roam free around this sea-land ball,
as the human accident lays at home,
Or in a hospital wing in crawl,
on life's floor of stone,
And yes, all hindrance paid off,
with a holiday in the sun,
like the light sought by moths.
And from the hospital wing they eagerly stray.

I see the politicians
bickering upon their fresh tailored ties,
Of morals and their position,
like stars that scatter themselves
about the skies,
They better each other in their promising shine,
to shine brighter than how they did in 2009,
Place your bet wishes upon me,
but what you get is not what is seen,
But when we get, it is our discovery,
like realising the use in what has gone,
Only when that bastard with iron heart,
has departed, can we embark
upon recovery.
And through a dystopian age, we
must remain so strong.

Television, why do we
pay money and attention,
If we did not,
we'd take a prevention,
I direct the hose of water upon the
fire so hot,
Before it spreads like butter.
Before life as we know it, shatters,
Before our lives are in the gutter,
Mind, we will all meet Death,
so what does it matter?

Temptation

The temptation of Christ,
t'was Lucifer's form,
But mightier was the Lord,
for of temptation he scorned!

But such gullible Eve,
whom subjected to fall,
By the beast of her he seized,
as the bait to maul!

God hath ordered his
gift to earth not eat,
Those fruitful fruits,
for it will be that of Death
they meet,
or lest, be the cursed acute!

And the serpent hath
insist to Eve, she devour,
Those Godly fruits of Eden,
that they will not make of
her, sour,
That the beast ordered she
heed upon,
The opened eyes of her,
for good and the evil
she will know and serve!

That Angel of Death

Bolted upright,
I don't want
that Angel of Death
to snatch my soul,
The back of my head is light
upon a heavy headboard strong,
I've every part of me left,
and nothing lost; nothing to owe
that Angel of Death.

I will not succumb to a temptation
that will rob me of breath,
I will not for a time
great or small, lie down,
This is my careful declaration,
signed by a sweating hand wet,
The blank void of mind I will sign,
and my identity; as not to lose it
in night hat and dressing gown.

"I, sleeping perpendicular, making a right angle,
will not become some a hundred and eighty degree,
for an Angel of Death to snatch my soul away from me . . ."

That Monster Cain

"That monster Cain,
that poor wretch Abel,
His deathly pain,
my creation met fatal!"

Jealousy! O' what hath thy done!
The murdered body,
I dragged and strung!
There is no solace upon
this earth, for that man,
A man of whom; my brother,
no, none will understand,
Why I killed him, so,
I protest he was better,
and so he had to go!

I bore enchanted fruits,
but God intended those
To remain upon the tree,
the hanging baskets of Eden,
As untouched as the rose,
whose intriguing redness warns,
We are not to reap the forlorn,
to give to one who has infinity, all,
For he hath forbidden them to fall,
in capture of human hands,
on these precious, young lands.
I, cast off from God's look!
The consternation I suffered hard,
as I anguished and shook,
There is no solace upon this
earth for I,

A man of whom bore competition,
in the eye of one not blind,
But the perfection of thy brother,
who bore his born cattle,
he, the knife of the cutter!

Yes, he succeeded in deeds,
poured out from beneath
his worthy bosom,
Unlike I,
I might as well hath herd them,
My brother's cattle,
unto terrifying battle,
I am lest, the corrupted being,
so foolish to think that God
was not seeing,
My shameful coldness,
and I am cool,
my body ghost less!

And I will spawn such
generations,
through Henoch, to Lamech,
Through bigotry! Incest!
And banish such revenge, and
unto me,
for it to be taken!

The Awe of Fragility

O' wonder! O' power!
Wandering mind taking
body form,
The greatest computer
we've ever known,
The keyboards are
our moist-soaked tongues,
The severing of heads,
and the hearts they pull!

O' surreal!
The greatest camera
through which we see,
The memory lanes and
trauma roads,
Freshly burnt images that
neither die of the cold,
Neither erode through
the age of time,
No matter how many soles
take a stroll through our mind!

O' unthinkable!
A human mind cannot be gained,
we cannot take of another,
All and our own cannot be feigned,
like the younger of his brother!
Although without gain,
we are susceptible to losing,
Our stringent sanity amidst
the danger of reality,
And all the while, a relentless
world keeps turning!
O' delicacy! O' fragility! The
produce of the feathered-flyer,
Rested in the curved bed,
held by a sports child "trier",
The race for life with the
speed and pace,
To catch up with our mind,
before the egg falls to lay,
cracked from some height!

The Castle

Crawling back through creation,
disorientated and eaten away,
Tumbling through the vault of
denunciation,
Back into the archaic grey,
turned to a face of clay!

Once fond of castle building,
here are the decrepit remains,
One of two minds killed in,
it's difficult to remain the same,
As the evil fades the sane!

The castle is particle and dust;
the debts are being paid in full,
A cracked, empty cup,
of what was once nearing full!

How can a visionary live in an
abraded home,
No shelter to stop the down pour,
a visionary so alone,
and sombre to the very core.

The Chorus

I

The chorus of my life be:
"O' beggars cannot be
choosers,
The ones of hate,
o' life's bitter losers,"
And I begged for a
life of independence,
And I chose a life
of which it renders
Me of all personality,
such is fatality,
In this dreadful life,
one alive with the chirruping
winged birds,
Can endure a death,
and live to tell its tale,
It's near absurd,
a string shortened,
Whilst it grows in length,
a major blip in its development,
And my major fall at life's hedges,
make of me melancholy,
A race horse loses its race,
makes my life of sentimental
pledges.

II

The chorus of my life be:
"A promising future ahead
in God's Holy land,
But yet I beg of Death
to take hold of my hand,"
O', I begged for success
once upon a time,
When the world was magnificent
and its secrets were mine,
But the world became vulgar
to my searching eyes,
The world's corruption of lies,
and people who led lives
so tasteless,
Who in spite, wore their masks,
who were truly faceless,
Beneath this masquerade
stood a pathetic breed,
Bred from falsified seeds,
whose green leaves,
Of arrogance and corruption
entwined,
Are of what they wore on their
hotly-ironed sleeves,
The true heart tucked away in
the forgotten attic of their minds.

III

The chorus of my life be:
"The empty page is not,
when it is labelled so,
We are not amongst the highest,
when we drop so low,"
For when my body drops
into sorrow's abyss,
Through deepest vaults
I endlessly travel,
There is no ground floor,
and dare I were to reach it,
Sorrow would be demanding more
of me, thirsty for my tears,
But I cannot produce,
nor let my sadness run loose,
Through brackish streams down
my cheeks,
This sadness is worse,
and no such relief,
I am decaying down to enamel
and bone,
Maybe I too wear the mask,
but I wear it alone,
There is the difference,
and all I seek is deliverance.

IV

The chorus of my life be:
"I do not rob others of
their precious health,
No, not those,
but of myself,"
I am the only friend of
myself,
And yet I betray and rob
of me my treasured health,
I succumb to Evil; its
persuasive technique,
And I, all alone,
it is solitary I seek,
Like the blind folk who
seek ignorance,
To make them that little bit
impaired,
They say a problem halved
is a problem shared,
Well, I have no one to share
life's awful blows,
And yet, I do not deny and
meet life's awful lows.

The Croon, The Voice:
Those Creative Rebels of Rock

The voice makes ends of words,
the breath, the aftermath, the afterwards,
Link, blend, sink into the beginnings of
the words that follow—
So effortlessly, as if he talks like he sings,
second nature to him,
Like the Sun finds it second nature to
bleed before the clouds,
Sacrificing itself upon the air
like a martyr, though this is temporary,
Sun was reincarnated into a new Sun,
given a new body,
Given a new soul,
though every day there after,
It combusts spontaneously to the surprise
of clouds half-dead on their mundane ritual.

The voice croons, with content absurd,
I can't take the absurd; I am full of it and could
Manage a brand new voice which holds its sin of
not conforming to messages easy to digest; sorrow
Of the other crooners who talk melodically of love things,
frantically pulling apart their limbs,
And hoping you'll do the same, and you
do it so mindlessly, yet you have not found
Your piece of mind, like the fair
have not found their rewards for being so; sensory
Though heart is not part of it; the lies have begun,
like the resurrected corpse of the Sun—sorry . . .
I do not listen to a master,
more of a guide of how to write my poetry, suffices
For my attitude that gorges upon mouth's creative residue—
God bless those dancing tongues.

The Dark—Its Triumph

I

The river unfolded like
a lucid, immeasurable
span of smooth ribbon,
And the nucleus of sick
yellow,
In suspense of the bluest
of skies,
Shone through my heart
like burning fire
Taking me apart,
one afternoon,
And despite the goodness
of an enlightening Sun,
The darkness of me
had surely won,
With lugubrious
sinking,
Unto my chest, of happiness, I
am dubious,
Lest—
I shall become
a thinning shell,
With nothing to tell,
of my venture unto gloom!

II

Opening the doors of my
soul,
O' there is nothing there,
It is none other than behove,
and is fittingly fair,
In my state of Depressive
languor,
Where all colours run down
paintings black,
And I can neither start another,
nor make my way back,
Through this darkened alley,
and I shall only paint of suffer,
In this sombre gallery,
of men with head in hands,
And a band of brothers,
in grimace and anguish,
Or the woman who doth languish
in helpless sorrow,
Upon the bed of yesterday,
and of now, and tomorrow,
Yes, she is bed ridden,
all fire given,
To make all rooms of her soul
ash and dust!
Where flames are killed
in wind's deathly gust!

III

And the dark has defeated
the passionate flames,
Man's life becomes the bane
of happiness' lutes,
And Man's own bane must become
an arrangement of flutes,
To serenade the sea,
that lonely gathering,
As lonely and lonely go hand
in hand,
As a sandcastle doth stand
upon some sands,
The wind's deathly gust,
will blow it away,
And it will fade into the night's
grounds,
Like the shying day,
well, the troubled shall lay
On the debris of what once was,
and they are doomed,
There is no underlying cause,
other than the curse
God has cast upon them,
when in life, when
They were enjoying joy,
and crying for sadness,
But a new found gladness,
when they saw the Sun,
When Sun created a beautiful place,
Lined with silver,
each cirrus of the sky,
Laced with pride,
those soldiers that marched on by.

IV
Well, I am here to admit,
there are no candles lit,
In my fractured world,
crushed with self destructive hands,
Watching blood seeping through life's
cracks,
Well, I am here to say,
that without the night,
there is no day,
And darkness spurns our
fantastic force,
The heart is our passion,
the mind is its source,
And well I confess, I have
the darkness,
But alas! There was once light,
before there was dark,
And there was some song,
before the death of the lark,
And so, when dark shrouds our
being,
It is only a matter of due course,
before the darkness; its dialogue,
Becomes the light we are seeing,
and all darkness will fade,
To Hell with its feeling,
replaced instead, with a secure ground
To bear our weight,
our love, our hate,
And a halo above our heads
will compensate for the damage in
Our ceiling,
made by the darkest times!

The Death of Moses

I

Both soles upon the
soul of God,
That incinerating pulse
of everything from the
silence of dust-clad lulls,
Unto the bushes of fire
he strode,
And upon the mountain,
across the stretching plains
of Moab,
The dying breaths are
counting,
The emerge of the blackened
crow,
A silhouette a foot the
dawn's burning sun,
Of where un-dimmed
eyes,
Fed off of the day that
had begun,
Of where he knows
he begins to die,
Beneath the Heavens
above.

II

A hundred and twenty
years of the past,
In which the Lord
hath seen all his life,
His service to His people,
that could not last,
An eternity long in
Lord's clocking sight,
Lord's loyal making
of an aged long faith,
The covenant to be broken
by half an eighth,
Of the ones before,
And this sworn land
Moses sees,
Passed down like
clothing,
Abraham, Isaac, Jacob,
and now Moses,
To collapse and seep
through the land's open arms,
Unto the soil's lonely weep,
hushered down in music
of final psalms.

III

Children of Israel
in child-like mourn,
Thirty days engulfed in
Moab's wide plains,
The plains of a child's
growing heart,
beruffled and torn,
Dressed in cloth so inane,
like the cloth of
that man,
Buried in Moab's valley,
starved of water,
Found in a child's tears
that ran,
And unto the soil in
ally,
With the pain of loss,
and out of a living
child's anguish,
Born is the essence of
the free man,
And he doth
re-emerge from Death's
sick languish,
Unto the shrouding
angels' wings,
Re-born in the soil,
to ascend from Death's
mighty sting,
And Joshua will
succeed him,
Unto God he will
turn loyal.

The Devil of Me

Resist; my dignified
defiance against that
Devil-temptation,
but we are always so biased,
When we point our crooked
fault bone digit,
Covered in years sinning skin,
made so flexing as any string,
To carry out everything
so damned and wrong,
At our own Devil-temptation,
is it not a Devil we
Feed inside of us,
with poisonous apples,
Or when we drink life's
intoxicant by the barrels,
And get mostly drunk
on our own immoral ways,
We had the intention,
and no morals stood in our way,
Well, we breed defiance out of
sin,
And the good must triumph over
the bad in us,
Temptation—now that is us,
a devilish thing!

The Human Perihelion

I am circulating myself,
There I am; all tip of the nose
and a furrowed brow,
Head cradled in cupped hands
at the table,
And I am contemplative of
my life, alone.

If this the breakdown to
silence all others in form
of communication,
I am at the beginning of
the human perihelion,
And I feel an overwhelming
trance of separation.

I look upon myself looking for
answers,
But I am looking in places
that they cannot be found,
The texture in the table; gauging
out my eyes and placing them in water,
The answer lay in observation of
oneself,
But we are at too much a distance,
and I continue to circle around
This person sitting at the table,
in helpless frustration.

The Incarcerated

Those eyes pierce my own
and make of them tearful,
And I am fearful
of them; I do not know
What else goes on,
are they an angelic pair of windows,
that can do no wrong,
Well, life has confirmed
one's suspicion,
That those windows with
darkest hue gaping through them,
Are prisoners dressed in dark
garments with life's glimpse of colour,
And can hold one to submission,
and we are left with some
Immobilizing envisions
and are turned to stone,
With those eyes stabbing a
man to his bloody death,
Or watching an innocent become
a convict,
In sky blue dress,
that those shameless sphere
people,
Incarcerated in those windows,
shall slowly, deviously lift,
To meet that of the convict's,
and blink in some understood code,
As if to suggest,
they are sending the innocent down,
And will watch the incarcerated drown,
in their windows' water abundance,
Rims of windows;
floods the window ledge,

As streams flow down the edge,
of interrupted cheek bones,
Well, I'm sure he would have known
those Devil eyes,
Or for when the windows are thrown
some rock,
Watch the glass crack,
and watch the incarcerated flock
To the scene,
in bitter rivalry,
Could make a man die on his soles,
an anxiety-crafted dream,
In every age,
we learn to know.

The Ivory Towers

There was such a group
of misfits,
All were writers,
all contained that creative cist,
And when it burst,
the copious writing began,
Upon some old parchment,
or they decorated their
Ivory Towers' walls,
with verses and metaphors,
And it was the law,
where all demons and angels call,
To be wrote upon and about,
dress them up in words and
Mount them upon the skies
in benediction, pleading out
From one's cunning enigma eye,
they were mysterious to others,
Not like their sisters and brothers,
in some dire age of struggle,
Where poverty-stricken masses
would, in darkness, huddle,
And craved for similitude,
and warranted their banal,
uncharacteristic ways,
But those up in their single
Ivory Towers,
Though synchronised mutters,
they were not the same,
The passing of days,
the passing of ways,
Those wistful, poor souls,
some might say,

But they've no insight,
none, not at all,
They do not hear
the words that call,
From their fireplaces,
and from darkest spaces,
And poets in their Ivory Towers,
will die with nothing,
Except with words,
those language powers,
Through dying of the times
they heard,
And they will leave a legacy
of notes upon walls,
In the hope that one day,
all the banal will hear their calls.
So that to be a poet,
will be a growing, barbaric breed,
Raging with tongues and pen,
those powerful words!

The Limits of a Dust Pan and Brush

A dust pan and brush, to sweep
away the errors
Like the ash upon the carpet—
that regretful addiction,
Or a place's dirt you brought in with you—
that regretful errand.

How dare they make
my life all ail,
Begot my life
of a bed of nails,
And the belly of the house
is caparisoned and divine,
How could they have
thought such a life was mine?

You cannot use a dust pan
and brush,
To push
away the fuss
And deception they caused,
or tear-laden eyes,
You cannot sweep away
a destruction's source!

The Meaning of Life

Seeing preview
is not seeing,
As a life of one's mask
is not being,
As obligation to believe
is not believing,
As snatching one's desire untimely,
is not receiving,
As a bird without its wings
is not fleeting,
As glancing from a distance one's fear
is not meeting,
As one who hath impatience
feels life
has no meaning,
And it does,
and they are wrong,
And they adjust to a life,
incognito,
The stems of incomprehension
and ignorance entwine,
Like the hand of mine,
in the hand of its other,
Doused in finer wine,
to seal this self covenant,
For those impatient,
I am confident,
Like the clasping of both hands,
like the merging of the sands,
I am confident,
for those impatient,
They are assigned
to a life of worry,

And in earth's sands
they bury,
Their hollow heads,
For in a life full of meaning,
they are impatiently led,
To conclude there is none,
when their actions are not rewarded,
When they seek reward,
and I am confident,
That they shall meet the Lord,
sooner than they think,
Sooner than one who cannot swim,
can sink,
through one colossal sea.

The Nature of Nature

On this humid evening,
I sat there only peering,
At the luscious tufts
of grass,
On a day somewhat overcast.

The Sun recoils above us,
trying to stop the clouds
that suffer us,
Denying our sun ray lashings,
for the clouds that strongly mask it.

The trees that exhale their
unwanted air,
The life they live, they
have to share,
To us, the superior human
kind,
This pact of give and take—
we are assigned,
To the fluctuating sooner and later,
to the nature of nature.

The Next Junky in the Confessional Box

Anaesthetize my spirit,
heroin will lift it,
Out of my heart,
out of the dark,
Into the fluorescent strobe
and flashing segments,
I'm a Virgin Mary,
glowing of the brightest purity
There is, and I confess to be
glowing of insanity all at the
same time,
But the universe is mine,
let me press my fingertips
To the faithful stars,
I have authority enough to
halt the cars,
And erase my scars
of life, blood I have not bled,
But of white power instead,
extremities of human emotion,
Stifled out of influenced notion,
but I can't contain
The alien in my brain,
a freak becomes of me,
An Imposter too,
but I am religious,
I am all religion and I made it
all, and I confess to be
Blinding of the Sin at the same
second,

But it was the angels, who beckoned,
let me answer their prayers
To bless them with divinity,
I have right to impose,
upon the world-facility,
Habit catering vicinities,
to restore joy in human anatomies,
Albeit, a long term catastrophe.
And make me be
a flying bird of sort,
To reach my goal,
that this habit has fought,
Because . . .
I just can't do it anymore.

The Road Taken

Two roads posed in front of
my view,
Like ourselves in passport
booths,
And if only then I knew,
from belated, sinister proof,
The saddening, harrowing truth,
that evil mind doth do,
To my fearless, stubborn soul,
its potential to shift and move
Violently the courageous heart,
to reduce one's courage to start,
To a cowering, lonely creature,
and of which one's paper is
Permanently marked,
with inerasable misery.
Because one of two roads I
chose,
I thought so naively there was no
difference,
And I did not ponder to pose,
that life-deciding significance,
To why one road; to Hell it goes,
and would beg of me deliverance,
And I in turn will beg,
for the walk to be reversed,
But that this responsibility shared,
is made for us damned and cursed,
And that into harmful, troubling waters,
so hot, we will surely burn,

And become at one with waters'
drowning, bad inferno,
Of which we won't return,
and this road; made to make
these journeys unto damned,
And thus; remnants of goodness I
must forsake,
On the road leading to unspeakable
lands,
The other road was not meant
for me and my foot that make print,
And this place by foot I was sent,
I have not seen footprints since,
The place where time is drunk,
where disorderly pendulums are,
Where one's heart is permanently shrunk,
and one's humour in a jar,
Pendulums regularly cackle
like gunshots in the trenches,
And I cannot escape this personified
fear,
I am in a losing battle,
And now such difference is crystalline
clear.

The Serpent Poet

If you could take a
gander through a poet's lens,
The mammoth kind of serpent,
its skins it sheds,
For a poet, it is
those words of verses,
Of which he cancels,
and sheds his worst ones,
And takes his stances
in contemplation,
Until a fresh replacement,
takes away from him
his procrastination!

If you could take a
meander through a poet's river,
The mammoth kind of serpent,
the invertebrate that slithers,
For a poet, it is
his flowing of phrases,
Of which he dives,
and through the water he raises,
And direction he changes
in contemplation,
Until he lowers the anchor,
which takes from him
his indecision!
If you could take a
wander through a poet's mind,

The mammoth kind of serpent,
whose scales of him that define,
For a poet, it is
his talent,
Of which he is oblivious,
through his hand-writing—gallant,
Who indulges in his pallet
in contemplation,
Until the colours that paint,
which take of him
a poem's completion!

The Wooded Landscape

Barks climb through the sky,
or so it looks from a distance,
And a lake reflects a rude awakening;
the ground lays dead and dried.

I see through one's eager eye
a debris of woodland murder,
I see it through one's inquisitive look—
the disease out of barks' contagious burdens.

Lend my shoulders to carry the dead
and why—
When it looks not part of I from distance,
when the lake reflects woodland's
Spirit in pressing state,
I do not want stain upon my
existence!

Barks climb to the filthy lake,
or so it looks from distance;
My despair—the rude awakening,
is exposed through
Despair of landscape
I trace . . .
In melancholia of states . . .

The Writer's Paradise

Turn my sleeping quarters
into paradise,
Make my home some old
manor,
To float up some staircase
weightless,
That creates home's heights,
and my literature room with
fluttering banner:
"This will more than suffice",
to spend my seasons in manor life,
O', so many reasons
for shutting out Winter's
Breathing and snowflake splutter,
and those branches that lash out,
As we thoughtlessly drift through
seasonal gutter,
And they lash out at ice winds
that mutter,
Murmuring their discontentment
at coldest hours,
And they mutter:
"I am here, 'til Spring takes over,
then I shall be leaving you
with February's daffodils,"
And yes, the prelude of Summer,
but still, I shall remain mummified,
in homely state,
Wrapped in spacious room of
floral clad wallpapers,
And old Daily Telegraphs,
like ardent sailors,
Aboard their ships,
they never leave,

They are in homely state,
and on Christmas Eve,
They are at sea,
And I, at manor,
and the grandfather clock
serenades me,
And makes me aware of the
time I do not see,
Well, it does not matter,
time flying or short,
With this paradise, I have been
bought,
And sold to the boldness
of the written word,
And gaze I shall into
vermillion embers of historic
flame,
And write as i watch,
and it means the same,
At my antique desk,
with bird's feather clutched,
Between thumb and finger,
I lower into darkest oil substance,
And write from mind,
that is there to govern us,
In life and in death,
and we abide by the law,
That we think whilst we breathe,
before our writing becomes
eaten in soil,
United with I,
for when I doth die,
It shall die too,
without one's will,

I pity that fool,
A long time before our time
reaches the closing chapter,
We must always do,
and pass our legacy upon the
ones,
Before those blights make a
lunge,
At our left behind life,
that we could not carry on,
And when the paper and I
doth die,
We shall complement one another,
in Death's flowers' bloom,
But do not write my paradise off,
do not say I have it no more,
For I will make sure I doth
carry it to Heaven's parting waters,
And shall make a new paradise
upon its shore,
O', I am sure,
that I shall exist in a writer's paradise
forever more.

Things Not Done

Know not of affection,
I have never loved,
Know not of the ground,
for I have flown above,
Know not the blooming,
I have never flowered,
Know not of the fear,
for I have never cowered,
Know not of the truth,
I have never seen,
Know not of the seriousness,
I have never been,
Know not of a dream,
or so I thought,
Infatuated with my day-dreams,
of which I had so willingly bought,
Oh! So very conned,
I feel I've lost
the very spirit,
That I hath cost!
And all is nothing,
and all I have lost!

Third Junky in Line

My final exodus,
an android taking a brief
dip to make of it rust,
This is my brief journey
through worlds unknown,
Making dirt of my blood,
and the induction into
normality, I suffer all alone,
Normality pains me like
my crown of thorns,

"No I won't do it again . . ."

And the thorn in my side,
but a dent in my pride
Is worth it all, for minutes
of strange perception,
And if anyone makes an
intervention,
In my perfect stage,
I will fall,
and I will fall alone,
Shivering sensation in my
bones,
Foam dispersed from my lips,
sacrificing myself to the
no-go zones,
I need these bricks of fix,
to build my hope,
on a downward slope.

Time

The mysterious time! Where does
it hail from,
Where does it go to, never-ending,
So short with joy, with contempt
so long!
They part hands so soon, for
contempt to settle in,
It's drawn out chimes!
They echo, they strike,
the height of our lives,
The faceless time of sight,
but of numeral, hand and
might,
The mysterious time!

The mysterious time! Why does
it dictate so,
As far as there is existence, every
second,
Made from God in his highest
abode,
He controls those hands, with
costless power,
Those lively chimes!
They speak, they light,
the darkness of trite,
The mysterious time!

To You (Mother)

Roses are complicated,
but intensely passionate,
Violets are our skies at dusk,
but as much as a gyration of seas,
And although the orris-iris brings
about our necks the scent of musk,
You mean as much to me,
and if anything—more,
Than what these rooted creatures
could drop and pour,
And bow at my feet,
through Summer evenings,
Or as I gaze supinely as they
spritely soar,
Making of me much less
or something more,
But you,
you bore me into this world,
Inside of you,
Months spent tightly curled,
inside of the womb,
But you,
who makes that sadness blue,
For you add to a great sorrow,
a lighter hue,

But you, you
make that beauty truth,
But you, you
who gave me life, and then
Spurned me to write this
with eager pen,
And a loving heart . . .
I love you,
and my love for you
Is no dying art,
as timeless as glass,
Well so are you,
and, I love you.

Vantage Point

I stood on some small hill,
and I had everything in view,
And the lament of a midnight chill,
made constant talk in the air of June.

With some amulet I wore,
to bade farewell to the Devil,
The evil that I saw,
was all about my level.

Ornate in Catholic values,
I began to proffer some moon
with faith,
For he is only silver,
and for belief, he came too late.

Imbue him with copper and gold,
and hone his secret eye,
So that then he will behold,
some religion before he dies.

Up in a midnight sky,
where all ilk of creation doth lie,
The sun and moon; at separation they live,
but then . . . they always die.

Vitula Sweet Music

Pulsating rhythm of sweet
Vitula,
Guttural trills,
forcing one's soul in one's
feet,
One's body complete,
a sentimental mover,
Over the hills,
I heard a sound no truer
than that of sweet Vitula.

Harmonious drones; horse
hair of bow,
Swirling notes,
stirring one's soul
in rose red nutmeg,
Making of one as whole,
as whole as one can get,
My soul furrowed,
with Vitula's coarse coats,
My heart; a filled burrow,
by the rush of horse hair bow.

My sweet Vitula, sweet music,
soothe my soul,
And caress my heart,
with a timeless art,
As that of sweet Vitula,
a sentimental mover,
Moved me while I sat,
Pounced upon my shell
like a cat,
Took me by one foot,
and then by the other,

Stepping fervently,
thy enlightened brother,
There is a hill that converges
with the stream,
Let thy stream of thy conscience
make thy dream,
And if a dream is but that,
and nothing more,
Let me indulge in passion's
desire,
And let my sweet Vitula take
thy soul; take mine essence,
And sprinkle it upon a
paradise,
And make of me renaissance
from thy dreams,
Make one feel reborn
from music's realm,
And make one's conscience
consistently free,
With sweet Vitula,
soul's sentimental mover!
I am one with the strings,
I confess I am redeemed,
Those beautiful things,
dressed in coffee coats,
The magic one hears,
of those pitching notes,
My sweet Vitula,
music to one's cold old ears.

Vivaldi Music

Intensity; violin bowed
in heat of the time,
Red passion fury like
a heavy-bodied wine,
To transform us;
erratic runs of blood,
Sudden Mr Hyde,
but slowing down now;
Turn your heart's beat low,
shallow, incubating song and
Of which lasts no longer
than of one lightning bolt we know,
And our hearts are shot
by the arrow; it carries "passion",
Each sudden musical flash and
we sink back into our bodies like
disappointment,
Life's heavy ointment Sorrow,
saturates us into the new dawning
of tomorrow,
But just when we write off our
glee,
Like the imprisoned once free,
beauty in its multiple strings,
Lifting, sinking, lively
old things!

Power to move us,
power to guide us,
Power enough to allure
us into shameless times
of the electric soul,
Unnatural, I know,
the Frankenstein of us,
What is to us dead,
what is to us
somewhat alive still,

Well, all beat like a marching
band,
In regime drills,
our soul on fire,
With heart's unrelenting desire,
oh, I know it well,
When soul, heart and ego
begin to swell,
At phenomenal pace,
Sir, you've got good taste,
Consuming the full-bodied orchestra
of gradual progression and haste,
We know it today as "existence",
of the human race.

Walks Through The Elements

Should I walk through
furious, feral flames of auburn,
To burn to ashes all of life's horrors
I have learnt,
And should I run through a
vast, violent volume of ocean,
To saturate body and soul in
life's cleansing potion,
To wade agile through a vigorous
ocean,
To defeat life's thickest frictions
in fastest motion,
So that upon driest lands,
I shall wade through life's air
As if my life were a sprint and
wade through life's air
As if it were Winter,
in a flustered rush to find fire's
warmth,
To sought life's challenges
like the cheetah or leopard,
Whom sought their prey,
with pace like no man,
During the midnight of our day,
with bravery as thy weapon,
With that of the Crusaders, it is
akin,
And we can become them in
their masses,
If we are willing to defeat this often
elegance of Sin,
That deceitful wretch,
where between its lips, all facade of
good had been kept,
Inheritance!

That is all Sin is,
And so . . . let us sprint through life's
challenges,
Without asking gingerly,
if the time is nigh,
To take off on loyal foot,
we can take flight,
And break a torment roof,
and soar through the sky,
Like the aircrafts and the doves,
to fly through life as time flies,
This, my dear, is my only love,
a harmony between the time and I,
Time, it is all-knowing,
and it will never die,
But if we can fly life,
in places that are rife,
With bitter feuds,
and ones rude and crude,
We will grow our wings,
from blood-stained sides,
Of thorns of lies,
from a man's window eyes,
And venomous tongue,
But to grow one's wings,
our escape has begun,
To flee life's burden,
and to see truth suns,
And water Spring and Summer
gardens,

With joyous tears,
a new lease of life,
Devoid of life's fears,
let life fear us!
And in the years we are here,
let us show who we are,
The strongest defiance made
from mind, bone and dust!

We Call Them Roses

Fine, ready growths,
we call them roses,
Dressed in seraphic coats,
the coats of scarlet it
poaches,
From the blushing of cheeks,
of two sweethearts standing,
Eyes, averted to the roses,
while hearts of both demanding,
The lovely scent of rose,
be scattered on their pillows,
And everywhere their feet go,
amongst the stealthy willows,
In the distance far,
throughout the growing
seasons,
Below the midnight lark,
the roses, some of which,
Through every season,
bloom,
Through winter, they will stitch,
the fellow flowers' wounds,
Who mourn the loss of climbing,
progression is the heights,
But in winter, they are dying,
perishing, stagnant,
in our sights.

Hybrid tears a plenty,
the colour and size of Hybrid,
The lengthy blooming,
sent Tea,
Throughout the season,
long,
The vigorous growth
that time bred,
That progresses in a romantic
song,
The rose,
our love,
Our symbol,
our life of love
that's nimble.

Where Be Flowers . . . ?

How do we vision a
world deprived of flowers,
All natural colour and
beauty truant,
Where be a tulip,
to match our Sun,
Where be the rose,
to present to one,
Where be the poppy,
to harmlessly symbolise
war,
Where be the sweetening violet,
to create a shade-enhanced
galore,
Where be the foxglove
to expose us to multiples
of pulchritude,
out from its strong, slender stem,
to accompany a solitary's
solitude,
Where be the bluebell,
to paint a sea on land,
Where be the primrose,
to remind us of the sifting,
delicate sands,
Where be the Lotus of the Nile,
what are Ancient Egyptians
to admire, not dead,
Where be the alpine to
grace a rock's bed,

Where be the pink,
to cultivate a garden
with timeless favouritism,
Where be the daffodil
to exist in a Spring's haven,
but isn't,
Where be the wilder rose,
To a Tudor, he is without
such a fair representative,
Where be the fish-hook
cactus,
To which all insects play
attentive,
So a flower that blooms
under our alluring, blackened
matter,
Can see Death's hand before
it brightens the day!

Written Upon My Stone

I'll be identified
upon a fresh-arched stone,
I'll be with all of the dead,
despite a life lived alone,
There is candour on
my stone,
And it translates into:
"I died alone . . ."

The earth emblazoned
with geranium,
Pinks, reds and whites
of Carpe Diem,
For I seized it,
and broke it in two,
And left behind,
the breadth of life I once knew.

Flowers so emetic,
if I were with the living,
Of freshly, heaving sickness,
I would be generously giving,
And I would unleash an
episodic contamination,
Upon my kind,
but t'would fill me not with
Satisfactory and selfish sensation,
to express my mind,
How it gorged upon the trifle,
of others' sickness I may find.

Beneath earth's protecting canopy,
my body doth lie,
And it is no more,
and upon me a wiltering sky,
We as one; we have been
a cowering weakness,
That none did see,
in our glory days.

My spirit doth lie sprawled
on the wispy, golden sands,
Life's wounds written on my
powerless hands,
And as I look beyond a brackish
tide,
The winds blow slightly,
watering my airy eyes.

The germinal was birth,
and now I am buried in the earth,
Of any worth, I hath never shined,
and my spirit doth make no
Footprint in lifeless sand,
and I am binded,
With the tidal waves,
and many tears I gave away,
That maybe I would
water plants and trees,
And God would grant me
the gift to see
Beauty I hath not been aware of
'til now.

Before I found myself here,
I heard protean whispers,
As from my chauffeur,
to a gaping hole I was taken,
There were not many changes,
there were not many there,
My shameful last ceremony,
to those it was shared.

I embroiled them in my death,
and my own musical ear,
Heard the cantata,
of the good and evil,
Serenading to me life's struggle,
and well, what does it matter,
They wrote me off,
from life all of a sudden!

(Children's Poetry)

A Butterfly Inspiration

Watch as the butterfly
flutters its colours,
But do not try to capture it
as a gift for others.

Let it flutter about
and above you,
But ignore not its symmetry,
those identical wings of two.

If this creature can match
its beauty on either side,
You can reflect what is hidden,
and learn to be kind.

Watch as the butterfly
flutters its colours,
And take its happiness,
to give to others.

A Rainbow

Doesn't that rainbow
speak to you,
From the indigos,
and yellows,
and ocean blues?

And how does a rainbow
come to be,
Those oranges,
and violets,
and grass greens we see?

The sunlight spears
through lots of rain,
The sunlight made of
every colour,
And the raindrops break
the sunlight up,
And every colour is revealed,
a far way up.

We think of the rainbow
as a multi-coloured curve,
But it can also be a circle,
so round and whole,
For when we stand
upon a hill,
we can see a ball
upon the air,
just an outline,
that is all.

And our moon can
make a rainbow,
Although it is so weak,
it shines of only sunlight,
from which the sun has leaked,
But we can find a
rainbow,
in every single day,
The flowers, the plants,
the people,
Colourful in their
own special way.

Colours

When I behold a rainbow
in my eye,
The colours of God arch . . .
are alive,
God, the painter of our
world,
The primary colours of
boys and girls,
In red polo shirts,
and stone-white shorts,
In flamingo pink dresses
and patent shoes of sorts.

When I behold a rainbow
in my eye,
The colours of God arch
across our sky,
God, the painter of
our earth,
And we pass on the colours,
around the earth we serve.

Stars, Moon, Dark and Shadow

The stars come out each
night for you,
And the moon, and the
dark, and the shadows too.

The stars await your
whispered wish,
They shine of your hopes,
each star you notice.

The moon awaits your
dreamy gaze,
It glows of elegance,
all night it stays.

The dark awaits your
curtains drawn,
So it can live
before the dawn.

The shadows await your
final task,
As trees will admire
the shapes they cast.

The New World

Your shoes can take you far
away,
To that place you really
want to stay,
Somewhere new, and full
of a fresh,
Questioning, excited, pleasant
guess,
Of "how?" and "where?" "How
far?" and "now?"
How do the farmers milk their
cows,
Or is it goats?
And what about boats,
How far do they travel
upon the sea,
On boat,
can I reach my wildest dreams?
And what about when
I return back,
How long will it take
for my curiosity to
unpack?

The School Day

When the alarm throws
you awake,
No matter the frustrated
protests you make,
It's time for uniform,
then for tea,
All ties and blazers,
"You've school, you see!"

The day seems as if
it will never end,
The books you've brought
and the pencils, the pens,
It's time for Geography,
then for Science,
All groans and sighs,
of your musical defiance.

But before you can look
at your Timex watch,
Or remember that morning
of the road you crossed,
It's time to leave
the school's haunting grounds,
And a sigh of relief,
at the bell that sounds.

(Sonnets)

Sonnets: A Collection of Depression, Controversy and Age

1

No dam to stop the depressive, gushing waters' doom,
a drought of all things I ought to do,
Too starved of joy; it's pleasurable feelings,
of inside me where all badness meet in,
Entwined in such inseparable plaiting,
an eternity it seems for which sorrow sat in,
For the happiness offspring who was unwell,
of no positivity I can lightly dwell,
Of no comfort in which I can bask,
as Depression wields its bewildering axe,
Making me a slumber on my soles,
the most wistful story ever told,
A certain pathos I feel for her,
an unexplanatory selection of which none can deter.

2

We are described as miserable when we choose to be,
an over reactive state of mind, of the sharpness we feel,
Of a sense of lost, of hopelessness, of despair,
when we surely believe life is not meant to be fair,
But I tell you this, that when we are miserable,
although we feel that life is abysmal,
There is abysmal none more so than the deeply depressed,
the lack of it; of hope, of desire, of our good and best,
The misery is but a mere, short-term discomfort,
but the horrible mystique lies in the depressive plum-foot,
For when we see a shade of purple, we see the confusion,
for how Depression's footsteps are our own—this illusion,
Hold up a mirror to your splintered mimic,
and discover there is no mirror image.

3

The slaughtering of our own kind draws us in,
to play attentive to the Crime of Sin,
We acknowledge the suffering; our sadistic inside,
we crave this exposure to expand our minds,
To fill our voids of thought with warning,
the incinerating sun that pulls through the dawning,
The permafrost floor that takes from us, direction
by securing out feet to make an aging reflection,
The murder and the macabre that stimulate our brains,
of that of curiosity that banishes the mundane,
When life is simply a chain of events,
for when happiness and beauty are always present,
Surely we are not the human form of sickness,
the most structured thing is made of crookedness.

4

I have not developed into all of such adult years,
although I have grown from roots from the earth,
Part of me is charged by impressionable trait,
the adult of me is still part faint,
Part of me, is taken by bygone times,
centuries of poets, and their perfect rhymes,
The adolescent of me still walks with me,
and the outspoken child pounces from behind the tree,
Through many years, I will become old,
but the child and adolescent will not be sold,
But when I pass over to Death's glorified realm,
the maker will take the years from the stem,
And I will once again be born unto this ghastly world,
and the cycle with repeat with life in the womb.

Sonnets: A Collection of Imagination, Art and Modernism

5

Imagination can be found in delightful things,
as joy is prompted to spread her wings,
But Man is as capable of as much sadness,
an artist who illustrates a human madness,
White can be covered with those menacing strokes,
a frustrated mix of which it evokes,
The pain of a human whom reveals their self,
for each one of our minds is a canvas stretched,
That can easily be tarnished with murky shades,
that conceal the dancing, fluorescence that joy once made,
The vermillion reds, and jealous greens,
overcome with grief, as darkness up heaves,
The mystical purples and river blues,
mind's normal emotions, symbolised by hues.

6

I detest this modernised world of ours,
intimidated by this time, where old age cowers,
Man has destroyed, and continues to destroy,
excessive recreation in which it dabbles and toys,
Interfering with our God given nature,
and behind all of this, shrill cries of a major,
And of a minor sounding thing,
exploiting the fall of Man, whilst to it, he sings,
Singing the words of shame and ignorance,
ignorance to his complacency, of what he calls significance,
He reckons he's serving our aging world,
bearing the mouth-watering fruits, the oyster's pearls,
We are all in fact, reversing through time,

using and abusing the gold of the mine,
Our quality of life is spoilt and cut,
it's time to close the technology door shut.

7

In our lifetime, we don't belong,
we chime to an age of different song,
An age plagued, by the deadliest disease,
this contagious Modernism we cannot please,
With traditional values that we givenly pass,
this disease making just, the splintered glass,
Of the mirror we point behind us,
in order to acknowledge the aged tusk,
Of our elephantine history,
the growth of society, and politics remains a mystery,
Our fantastic literature penned by undeniable greats,
who revolutionised this world with curable grapes,
Modernism has become, due to the old,
but has made the fire so hot, it's cold.

Sonnets: A Collection of Balance, Obsession and Alienation

8

An ability to reveal both an angel and a demon,
to show society's disciplined star and the bohemian,
To execute destruction and cure,
to witness a life of rich, and a life of poor,
An ability to show both one face, and another,
to be thy sworn enemy and a loving brother,
To execute an idleness and a production,
to apply to life both moment and structure,
To experience both a venom toward humanity,
and to demonstrate a penchant for the calamity,
That, in that we are as evanescent as the speed of our life,
and that we are the fleeting comets about a universal sky,
Of an equal balance, we are contemporaries en route,
and of an equal balance, we are born resolute.

9

In inclusion to the loner; there comes a time,
when in obsession, he is especially fine,
In that, he, will obsess over the evasive paths,
and only afterward, he will feel obsession's wrath,
Those in ethereal walls, he will sit in its centre,
and that he too, a recluse, is surely better,
For if he were to live outside the house,
the panic of life would surely arouse,
His incarceration, so he would run back home,
and about his floors he will solely roam,
His obsession is his everything; his epitome of existence,
as he's little power, and no resistance,
Unhealthy, yes, but to him not so,
into the realms of infatuation and obsession he goes.

10

There was a building I could not enter,
and the doors were barricaded whenever I went there,
I bombarded the letter box with copious paper,
and I committed to paper my alienation, for which it catered
For the words I had not spoke through tongue and lip,
and for this anxiety, I was left unequipped,
At this giant door, except for my handwriting,
panned into fighting,
With myself in torment,
and all the while, the progression lay dormant,
I sought to out manoeuvre the majority of those,
who into that building, those come and go,
And I lay supine against some wall,
then I realised I had left myself back home.

Sonnets: A Collection of Grandeur Delusions

11

A mind thrown into the spaces,
into territory of alien places,
He is with us; we are not within him,
there is only room for that profoundest of things:
The thought; what he has to bring,
the wrists in seizure; the neck that wrings,
Overtaken by the friends and the peers,
and his own destinies are colossal yet unclear,
He's made up of ideations; his concrete beliefs,
that his mind is the world; yet for this, he weeps,
He is special; he is the empire,
albeit, there is no smoke without fire,
And it is himself he intensely admires,
but that his mind needs to sleep for he is incarcerated in mental fatigue,
    and he is tired.

12

His mind laughs more than it cries the rain,
but there is no question that he is one of the sane,
And if this were questioned,
surely all laughter would be lessened,
To make room enough for the distress of embarrassment and shame,
for he will lose every delusion with all reality to be gained,
And what once was a grandeur delusion, bearing gifts of hope,
What stood in lieu; the reality, of which he cannot cope,
How the mind led him along the stretches of elation,
how he was led to believe he was a non-entity in his generation,
For he was human; yet he was not,
he was religion's uncollected relic and through life's cards of misfortune; he
    never forgot,
But reality he had, since,
he contained one who defined a human madness.

13

Two men facing opposite directions,
centuries' human breed by election,
And they are me, and I am them,
when the truth will be told, I can't predict when,
The single eye; this is mine,
I don't use two; I am all symbolism and sign,
I calculate coincidence and it equals reason,
I am not one to disconnect from them when all evidence leaves them,
When all evidence is lost, I bring forth my own,
to join the dots of life is my life-long goal,
I am the perception master of this age,
I am the undiscovered genius that God intended to make,
And he brought me forth unto this world of pain,
but my pain unearths the gift . . . of being insane.

14

I know I could defeat them purely on powers, I know I could,
though I relish in the ecstasy of being misunderstood,
They don't understand me, well neither do I,
and there are symbols and imagery in the clouds of the sky,
All for me, for I am eternally blessed,
it's a bit of fun, though they surely wouldn't have guessed,
That there's an imbalance inside of my brain,
and that all of this "fun" could seep in between the bars of the drains,
Into every one, let my heightened sense of being slip away from my grasp,
unlock the tight fists of my hands in tightest clasp,
And let those poor mites run free of me,
and of all those faces in my reflection I see,
I don't understand, this is infinitely real,
I've been dispossessed of true happiness, and only emptiness I feel.

Sonnets: A Collection of Narcissism, Self-Healing and the Curtains

15

I admire thy self completely,
O', and so very clearly,
I can see the shine of thine light,
the future is I; the look takes sleep in my sight,
Of a smitten face; smitten, I am satisfied,
an exceptional interest; it will never die,
O', I am in no shaking doubt over myself,
I, the priceless museums and galleries without thy wealth,
O', I am a pauper, and paper; on fire; I keep the fire hot,
no matter of the admirers I have not got,
The fire of admiration, I derive from I,
I leap into myself, before I tread the sky,
And well, I need not those books and text,
for I am simply the very best!

16

O', that my soul were a fine, crafted instrument,
O', the strings of my heart upon a harp so malignant,
The bow of my bones, in rapid motion,
and thine fluttering heart—a generous token,
For my heart, I wear on thy sleeve,
and the fabric becomes claret when I doth breathe,
But such downbeat music becomes but sweetness,
and I am enraptured in song, and generally needless,
A sorrow song doth stir my soul,
for the soul be an instrument I have always known,
Through my life's times pain,
and through such moments of mundane,
To make something so full of music,
and of the soul; it soothes it.

17

They hang like the weight-ridden chandelier of thy ceiling,
they hang like Death, devoid of feelings,
And if we choose, they close us in,
heavy, depressed fabric; does it fit in?
With an enlightening lamp and an image of walls,
and of a servant table, and the clock that calls,
They have as much life as a heart of stone,
and do not beat like a heart; not even our own,
For out of heart's blood taste, you brought them to this place,
yet they fall in pleat, scrunched into disgrace,
And shadows vandalise a darkly violent violet,
but those curtains, they hang through voice and silence,
They don't have feet on the ground; they are in indecision,
yet creating such awful, disturbing vision.

Sonnets: A Collection of Anxiety

18

Atmosphere, I can hear,
disturbing to one's human ear,
It's near deafening,
the greatest method that we seek no method in,
Sensitive ears, please don't wake them,
but you do (and if you do); damage is done,
The outbreak of war,
it hath begun; resilience thaws,
And all about this planet floor,
a puddle at my feet 'til I sweat no more,
We can mould the air like dough,
and of this intense anxiety, we only know,
To release pent up fear and tell it to go,
but yet it replied, and it said "no . . ."

19

Fret over the patterns in the floor,
that is me, and there is more,
To observe oneself whilst trying to focus,
a generous fraction; like the water that comprises of most of us,
I am a student and a hoard of inspectors,
I play attentive in my self-taught lectures,
Though, I taught myself of human vibrato,
I, the trembling, anxious, frightened Beethoven,
Composing fear,
the paranoia beat that is consistently near,
High pitched, low pitched, limitless worry,
myself in mind, I have buried,
With on-going sombre reverie,
and such life lived careless has permanently left thee!

20

Up the stairs' challenging blocks; turn a sharp right fast,
stumble unto Bathroom's arms, but it hadn't passed,
That wretched anxiety that makes of me,
a suspicious creature to all that doth see,
A fugitive on run for their life,
plagued with terror from anxiety's strife,
I could, where I stand, perish tomorrow,
basking in my own definitive sorrow,
For life's sharpness I have borrowed,
from the "what if" of foreseen tomorrow,
It hath cut deep like a kitchen knife,
my fast-paced disaster of life,
And this breath is mine all,
and it could be mine final!

21

Rumination of memory lanes,
brings to fruition life's mental pains,
Yes, it pains me like a knife of betrayal in my back,
existing in one's tragedy of a horrid past,
I am tragedy, my failings vast,
yes, derived from my sorrow's past,
I can count on one hand, my successes,
light put in the shade, as light confesses,
It's flaws laced with regret,
regretting the light of Sin it had met,
We talked, or rather, I lent my ear,
and I was placed in eternity's fissure,
Between a past and in being futuristic,
and the corpse of my life is foul, rotting putrid.

(Prose Poetry)

Clueless Travelling

I met this traveller, and he had walked the earth. His feet were stained with a blood red wine. I lent him my shoes, and he continued his journey. Comfort can allow us to resume our journeys, and this was evident, for he became some clarity disaster of a dot. By nightfall, I saw it no more. Was it the lack of a sun's light, or was my sight impeded by the distance he'd travelled since encountering my good deed? I cannot say for sure, it seems the case. But then again, anything seems, yet it isn't so.

I caught glimpse of some more dots; a lonesome desert's retinue; oh, how I wondered where they were destined for. A man's curiosity would not hurt no more than loneliness. You say that, but we travellers value solitude intensely.

I did not know my own destiny; the place with a time, but nevertheless, I continued walking beneath some starry sky.

We travellers, we seek nothing, we see all; the wide plain of sands, and a sky's gigantic palm of hand, from my vantage point.

We do not call our destiny, but it calls us under that patchy palm of hand, beckoning us, pleading with us to devote our attention to their pitiful state.

> Well, it serves me as some distraction from my own, of which is currently deplorable; I think I will answer my destiny's call. To serve as some companion for a few dozen laps of a clock's hands—that is all.

Compos Mentis

The cerebrum of our brains is like the barks of trees, and we cannot seize its centre, and take it home; the bevelled square we try to hone. It always manoeuvres unseen, out of our avaricious grasp, but we can obtain its ingredients from every sprouting branch, like a child artist who fears there will be no mystery of purple; to expose the mystery, to make some artist's history, they will soon discover that carmine and electric blue make a suitable hue!

There's a chasm in my world, but in years of duration I have learnt, that it is just a wound, and it can be concealed with freshness; a new beginning, that is what I have learnt.

I can be rid of life's pain I suffer, for a short while, when branches are broken off by culprits of my past, and what seems the right anodyne—codeine substance, I thought this would suffice. But this is not right, we must resort to becoming this thing, "Joy", as it so truly wants us; to convert despair to elation, we can co-exist with dark's trial of separation!

Our mind shall kill its matter, of which spurns the disease of sorrow, and trauma. Celestial brains burying the dead darkness, there is no difference, only that when it is alive, we become dead; a temporary discomfort, that drives us to the abyss, and back again through the circles of Hell, until we see worse off, and see how others splutter on cough on diseases far worse than our own—that Sorrow.

I am at one with sanity, though I will openly confess my chronic confusion, my life's chronicle of this maddening Sorrow—is it simply just, and only an illusion. For when I stare into darkness, into a Hell's mouth, I stare so hard I begin to see butterflies, and this I know, is the discovering of a colourful life, through my eyes. Black is made of all God's colours, and such yellows and pinks will eliminate that disease of darkness, after I have encountered the gruelling hardship of strife, in this otherwise wonderful life!

Concentrated Observation: Short Term Fixes and Questions

Companies since forever shortened their names into initials; called it "abbreviation". And I have, through many a company's contribution, realised how lazy humanity is. We always want the "easy way", we want the bus journey not the walk, the spoon but not the fork, the wine without skilfully removing the cork. Alleviation—a short term "fix" provides such an easy way as this, watching our hands and wrists wring energetically, realising they need not apply themselves to "work", and this short term elevation of the energy sets just above our heads like haloes, only by no means is this "the end"—there is no permanent escape, the energy floods into our minds like teeming, tepid rain that make tangled rat tails of our human hair. And it did not come late, the time for this was and is and will always be right—predict one's mind, analyse with the energy giving in abundance, is this the turning of a sharp, harsh corner for the sane? Do they succumb to the tragedy of insanity?

One Greek philosopher, Socrates, preached that the aim of life, was to "know thy self"—it is true man should judge another of his kind by his questions, and not his answers. It is so much so, curiosity conquers the element of response on the mind's hierarchy. To question, is to release and to expose to one, one's hunger prior to the hunt for knowledge. It is off one's own back, that the quest is made, even if the result of both processes in the mind, are by which we are led to, are what offer the same conclusion. Answers take no thought, answers can be obtained from the media, from the aid of modern technology, from the written fact in books—this is no use. We require a posing of our own words, of which will certify that what knowledge we are led to at the end of the journey, has substantially rewarding qualities in that we have worked to obtain, amongst other qualities of which include a priceless quality obtained from truth—to satisfy one's curiosity, to quench one's thirst for knowledge, to pave the road for which walks of progression are trod upon.

Destiny

The boat I was sailing capsized. Untimely, though so naturally—childhood's errors, and through to old age, it does not get any better. With such generous amounts of failings, I deserve to enter such oblivion with a mournful sigh—who knows what will gather, in one's naked eye. Maybe I shall see some people I once knew, and threw away hastily, like pebbles to the sea, just so my emotions could glow of a brighter hue. It was bright, but it was luminous, and reluctant to be there, though it had no choice—like all of God's stars, those shying dots, they've the black sky, that immeasurable canvas—what have I? When you realise there is nothing to conceal shame, nothing to conceal hate, nothing to conceal what we truly feel—the change. That is when . . . we deserve to die.

Fire in my Throat

The fire gathered in my throat, and I was forced out of myself by a conquering force of anger. And a burst of rage in the form of sound brought such a rage as this, to the ears of others. Oh, but they deserved it, they coaxed out this dragon.

It was an unintentional broadcast, and if it was not unbridled energy, I could have conquered it with some sense of knowing; of foreseeing; of being the occasional water hose bearer.

With the power of trickling water, had I broke out into a kind of sweat before this, I could have contained my emotion in a box, inside the throat, locked to everyone else; to suffer silently in common sense.

I had exhausted rationality with my hoarse cry, and all other words I had willingly prepared, had no other option that to die.

They did not get a funeral; I had no time for that. I had no time for anything, except for deepest, darkest rumination of thought. I have rendered myself of words, I have none left, what is the use, I am better of as dead. Just a hapless soul, with a small fire of anger, that spreads like butter whenever anger is aroused.

I have no control; no, none whatsoever. If someone gave me a gun, I'd kill them all today. All of the liars, all of those I despise with such a fiery passion called anger. I have no control, to preserve my reputation.
Give me something, and I'll see it done. And see it all the way through to the passing of my soul.

Hooded Supremo

All about the land struck an inclement reign of discouraging weather. How we lock our doors, and lock our temptations away, so as not to stray out into a sky's time of fury.

As humans, we can be discouraged, but often rebel against it, as proof we are free, that we conjure up our own freedom from discouraging discourage, and causing it near humiliation. We have the strength to admit we are sometimes indecisive, and our minds—ambivalent, no matter how wrinkled and worn we seem, our exterior—this means little; a home's interior means everything. Parties are not held outside a home; it in itself is welcoming on a cool and harsh Winter's evening.

I pulled up the chair—plain and old, a child's spray paint affair of black and white—and lightning made the black territory shine dark, and it made the white shine bright, brighter still, in comparison to the bolts themselves. They were some ill health of a pale yellow.—a downplayed lemon of streaks; weather decoration across the sky.

Well, I sat at the window for six days, and on the Sunday I rested. I refrained from becoming a watch man in relation to an abysmal inclemency of weather, from a sky's open mouth.

And I did not stop it, for I am looking down upon the sky. I, God, hooded in the clouds blasé shapes that I made.

No More

My identity is not my face—faces change. My identity is my soul—it is not accessible to the human eye. The well man can become a bruised man, but the soul is always well—our identity is concealed, and who is to say that our exterior defines us, it is merely glamour. Who is to say we are full of nerves, it is only our stammer. But my soul is not well, and the world—far worse. I was born with an ill brain, and it seems eternity, that I've lived this curse. I am dead. But I'm still here.

My diet consists of bread and wine—I devour the body that is mine, and drown my lungs in active blood, re-grow some more when my breathe shows signs of the flood. This is so . . . that motivation is murdered, so ironically, the blood is less; I drink no more, it does not prompt growth of understanding, lest I should become that all-knowing mess, who has all responsibility—I have very little. Brush my hair, brush my teeth, become the outsider, and watch myself slip away into cognitive reverie of agonizing torture—it's then the ambition begins to leak, and down the drain, upon the floor, across the carpet, my ambition—no more.

Out of Body: Induction to Imbroglio

It could have been sleep paralysis, but no—I was some body of hot larva, macerating the rough bed sheets beneath me, and they were pleading mercy. They lost dignity through my melt, they lost stiffness through my childish pouring of human matter, they were in cohesion with me, when all they wanted to do, was prevent my glass body's shatter; the protective fabric on which dreams are lived, and if I was awake whilst I was asleep, it would only bring imbroglio upon the snake-skinned sheets, too much a burden I could give.

During some stage of chrysalis, I was not liquidated child, easy to shape—pour it in front of some people, and watch it call with open arms. And watch it poured in front of a bookcase, and watch the unfolding of impressionable aftermath. Nor was I some fully-fledged adult, briefcase and financial affairs tucked under arm's wing, not a fully independent thing!

Every texture of the room's features, were accentuated to the point that I became the texture; some repetitive, oval's outlines inside, inside, like the naked eye's accessible Russian Doll—it's x-rays upon the furniture, time and time again! My tomb of the catacomb is buried beneath the ceiling, in inescapable confusion, unresolved anxiety.

My skin was chiffon through to my undeveloped bones! Cessation of secrecy, the exposure of my legacy, whilst still fully aware! And the lurid carpet stares in sight, and the lurid carpet stairs out of the light, but my room was in so much light, I became pig-headed to the point of insanity. Ignorant of reality, absorbed into the fabric of insanity, I know I will get an opportunity to look properly at myself, whilst zooming through a tunnel of endless, jumbled thoughts.

I became the chaplain; the daily visit, to my bed bearing the weight of the coma I was in. In clergyman white wear, white as snow, still not as white, and not as bright as God's light I have known!

I am for once, a competent soul, and I am in the knowledge, and with mental blast, into God's everlasting lantern of light I go!

Superfluous Youth

Uncouth—they all are, and all they will ever be to me. It is veritable I should call upon them to be cast away like stones and bottled messages to the sea; like she to he, when her family has disowned her, and washed their hands of her girlish foolishness. And she cast away like stones in the hands away from me!

Superfluous youth; they do not perplex me, rather they vex me with hate!

For when a smile doth occur, cracked on their visage of plastic, I will remain demur to their falsest of approaching, in my hatred state.

Their traditions loll like stressed curtains; touch a stepping ground, laying to be stepped upon by glamour converse boots, in their tedious territories all around.

But I relish in knowledge that their life is but an impasse—mine is like the growing grass; progress is made, and they will wade through my success. To trespass to envy, those jealous swine—I will not lend thee this success of mine!

The Decline

Aged, wrinkled skin; the epitome of their tiring life, tiring is an eternity of which it seems, clinging weakly to Arthritis-sickened fingers. The stiffness of contraction—the pain of change.

The ancient jewellery that still jingles, though a haunting, taunting ring of Death; an ancient break up of words, to such ringing, humming those golden songs.

So mature, they are in need; a help in hand; the warm company of another's breath.

The human decline, we see it in this pitiful age; maturity in the children, the experience trapped within . . . a retarded, bodily series of function.

The magic of youth, they witness it fade; stood up in the witness box, of their shared home; they see youth shrivel and die.

"When I was your age," they mutter in short, difficult breaths: "I was a bridge, for others' troubled journeys, I became a distance leaper.

There was nothing I could not do, but now I will succeed Death's place, the place of that last that died here in this old age sanctuary. And there will be nothing of me left, my friend."

The Repentance of a Killer

How could he sleep during the skylark's upward warbling, and how could his spirit begin soaring out of the earth's dimension—how could he dream? To dream so gayly, with lack of tension, a form of prevention against the tired mind, pleading for a sweet rest to banish all consciousness; the person and the monster entwined.

Guilt became a triviality, when really it was quite important, to mark us human. He felt no heaviness upon his breast, lest he would become a weakness, a parasite to his pity; that he would not have a hand in his power, a post mill would be propelled by convicting hands, of which turned his world out of all proportion, toward the setting of the sun—languishing in gayness of life, but only by a portion—that caught all unbridled energy, that marked his downfall, of where atonement begun.

No, atonement wasn't his cup of tea; an ounce of repentance, and all would see. Exploitation was not for him, no.

Albeit, perhaps he resorted to clandestine prayer, and blessed his former prey, of whom could not be there, of which would erase the need to pray. And perhaps all prey became cirrus, and whenever he surveyed the Heavens, he nodded in repent, upon his fallen brethren, of which had become some higher level, above the cursed beast of him.

"Nearer to God, further from Hell", the killer thought.

"My brother is all dressed in gold, with silver wings and translucent eye, that look upon the dying world, and of my specious neglect of remorse days gone by . . ."

"Perhaps, the instinct I bought, and the dead I sold, was meant so; how those ones of apparent virtue boldly go, but I have become a murderous beast, and of their devastating flaws I know!"

"When we are good, we see good in everything, from the wannest child, to the heart of stone, even when we are part ridden with some Sin; a self-righteous thing! But when we are filled with the bad, badness unto the rim—overflowing; Sin's abundant

brimming, we see the death in everything—in the emerald evergreen, that all their leaves are long gone, and by nature, so thin, that they are ill . . ."

"And we see hatred in every smile, every whimper in every laugh, and every glass full, is only full by a half—everything is deprived, just like the lives we took, to make of ourselves more memorable than do-gooders, and their prestige of human look!"

And when the killer fell into convict garment, the secrecy, he did not warrant. He had stepped lightly and sprung through marshes of which foretold his conviction; he wept during his sentence of which he had been given, and came unprepared with no dignified, protest of valediction.

He uttered in high pitch, and sung like the Australian wren that lulled him to sleep, one Winter's night. Yes, he became a distressed bird of song, in the eyes and ears of the convicting throng.

"I prayed every night from my vitreous panes that gave my eyes a glassy look, I cried tears of glass that no soul saw, I repented then, and forever more, save me! Do not carve into my clot of heart with a blighting claw, my delayed guilt!"

And the gavel came down upon the wood, upon the killers head, an iron hood, and he became no more, in electric frenzy—he, like God's new recruitment of angels, he saw. Every night.

We Stand Alone

Upon the mountains, we stand alone. In streets, beside fountains—all stand alone. Nothing and all, that we do condone—the extroverts' fears, and what's none more excruciating, than the fear of being alone.

Extroversion; the fire in the hands, and if fire is not passed in contagious friendships of sorts, they will burn. And they will suffer, for life's fire they have caught—the remnants of desire and smile, the lie of the distraught.

Introversion; the fire in the mind, and if loneliness is met, that fire will spread. They will gain natural fires of warmth, in some same old story of Winter—the sociability is dead, and solitude will heighten the soul—it will not hinder.

The silence; a ticking clock, the ear's nutrition and the introvert are on a diet of which is full of drafts, of which lacks fruition.

By God, I know how I stand alone, and in some chair, cutting me down to a smaller size, I stand alone. Alone, I've every confidence of all the speakers, but I place my thoughts (those words) in a shallow grave.

Oh, cure the human heart! The introverts dwell in their underground chambers, those wrought iron cells—their honest havens. And the skin is perpetually marked like the door ajar, time and time again—marked the room with silent flurry, a daunting atmosphere for any man, regardless of whether he swirls his pen.

Yes, this skin wears a frown, a false start; candidates that learn through suffering trial—their greatest art.

Wings

Their wings I have never seen; wings of a fine feather, masking the width of a person, with some deceiving pure white. They had murdered their kind, words and hands, yet no horns; only haloes. And angels? They had never been, the stroke of lightening and monster's growling, neither sun nor fine weather. And I stood from a fair distance, asking, whether or not to be certain—that my suspicions ought to be relabelled fact, not just a thought.

They were under the binding sky of freedom and cirrus, pacing permafrost ground with their bare, pale feet. And everyone owns wings, though of these in particular, I have yet to see them. And they probably own them, yet they live lives, led to kill and bleed us . . . of our experience profits. They capture us, hands grasping the fleshless air, 'til they find our own—into the feverish snare, frail and hapless, the transaction was somewhat silent and no one saw, no one gathered that murder had graced the world, again.

Some may say that the murder is just some delusion, and that I am deluded, and not to my knowledge, I acted out death. Well I offer some response, in which I can conclude it was my own wings that flew me to the scene, and this is the conclusion. And one's wings do not lie; do not take you to a time with a place, without good reason. And there is this blurriness of knighthood and murder, just some huge, complicated collage, its creases in the paper where glue has been sloppy, marked on my brow; like the season of Spring, and the season of Summer, that flood into one another in the span of a few months, flooding like estuaries into the river—their time of promotion.

So, looking hard enough, strenuously, as if I were trying desperately to build the city of ancient Rome in the mind without hands, I began to feel a little more weight on my shoulders. I am all but tough, and began dying again, only no one else was present with me, no murderous committee; some board of gentlemen and ladies on foot, I was completely on one's own. And I was on top of myself with puzzlement, with contempt—the murderers; they've got away with it again . . .

Suddenly, as if by self command to clasp in the hand the one shivering cold, the feathers of my wings were showering down in front of me like the ruthless, cold-hearted, cold-bodied rain . . .

Lightning Source UK Ltd.
Milton Keynes UK
UKOW01f2338181016

285623UK00001B/125/P